SONGS FOR THE SLOW LANE

For Johanna –

woodblock print –

sound of grasshopper

and butterfly

Hugh O'Donnell

Songs
for the
Slow Lane

the columba press

First published in 2014 by
the columba press
55A Spruce Avenue, Stillorgan Industrial Park,
Blackrock, Co. Dublin

Cover design by RedRattleDesign
Cover painting, 'First Day of Holidays', by Brigid Birney
Illustration by Evanne O'Caoimh
Origination by The Columba Press
Printed by ScandBook

ISBN 978 1 78218 148 4

Permissions
The author and publisher gratefully acknowledge the permission of
the following to use material in their copyright: Elizabeth Bishop,
Kerrie Hardy, Maire Heaney, Naoki Higashida, Michael Meegan,
Bernard O'Donoghue and Ciaran O'Driscoll.

Every effort has been made to trace copyright holders. If we have
inadvertently used copyright material without permission, we
apologise and will put it right in future editions.

Acknowledgements

The seed of an idea for this book was planted during a conversation I had with Pat Egan more than a decade ago. Pat was editor of *The Salesian Bulletin* and asked me to contribute a regular reflection on living with a new awareness of our place in creation and our responsibilities to the earth. A related theme soon clarified itself, namely, how to slow down our runaway lives and be in communion with all that is. *Songs for the Slow Lane* was born.

Prompted by the encouragement of many people, I have decided to gather up the scattered pieces for publication. They are all gifts in one way or another from the One whose love moves our hearts and moves the stars and who invites our response to the question 'where are you (hiding)?'

To the chorus of voices whose wise and generous words season these pages I am deeply grateful. To Aidan Mathews for accepting a number of these 'songs' for the radio series, *A Living Word*, my thanks. To my family and friends and to the wider family of *Crinan* – Salesians, staff and young people – may you be blessed. To Fearghal, Patrick and the team at Columba, may you thrive!

Contents

Spring

Springtime	13
Animal Presence	15
Five a Day	17
Horse Sense	19
Manners	21
Bookends	23
Tell me a Story	25
A Bit of Real	27
Listening Among the Ruins	29
'From Down Where the Hare Sees'	31
Prayer Plant	33
Silent Spring	35
Granny-in-Cork	37
In Memory of Her	39
Learning Without Accumulating	41
When Bad Things Happen	43
A Question of Size	45
Neighbours	47
Soil Mates	49
Cherry Blossom, Heywood	51

Summer

Brother Sun   55

Leaf Miner   57

Swings   59

Indonesian Rainstick   61

'You don't need feet to play football'   63

Dancer   65

Bundoran   67

Sea Campion   69

Herb Robert   71

The Man on the Corner   73

Three Little Pigs   75

Just Lingering   77

Corncrake and Cuckoo   79

The Singing Bird   81

Habiba   83

Sharing a Shadow   85

Elegy   87

A Taster   89

Coastal Sunset   91

Real Food   93

Autumn

Earth's Child-Face   97

Begonias on Sean McDermott Street   99

Let us Stop to Admire an Apple   101

Hare and Tortoise   103

What News?   105

At the Alliance Française   107

'Have you Caught Anything?'   109

The Holy Man   111
Laughter at l'Arche   113
Chinese Friends   115
Those Who Carry Pianos   117
Three-Legged Race   119
Beloved   121
Whistleblower   123
Soul Singing   125
Deaf Musician   127
The Fox and Prince   129
Street Mime Artist   131
Wake-Up Call   133
An Eyewash for the Eye   135

Winter

Baby Light   139
Earth's Begging Bowl   141
Geese Flying   143
Four Days   145
It is Finished in Beauty   147
Bud   149
What Love Does   151
In the Father's House   153
Darling God   155
Angels at St James'   157
Made in the East   159
Brógeen   161
An Post   163
Kinlough Stream   165
Tree Talk   167

Water Tables   169
Two Clocks   171
Scraps for the Feast   173
All the Time in the World   175
Snowdrops   177
One for the Road   179

Bibliography   181

Spring

Springtime

The spring equinox occurs within days of the feast of the Annunciation celebrating Mary's breathtaking conversation with the angel Gabriel. The significance of her 'yes' resonates with this two-step in Earth's dance around our Mother star, the Sun.

With its balancing of day and night, the equinox is meant to be a time of celebration, a time to reflect on the amazing universe to which we belong; the bigger picture beyond our local quarrels, our sickness and grief.

By 21 March the daffodils are well up, trees are deep in green thought, the earth is throbbing. It is also the season of Lent as we emerge from dark times and prepare to greet the risen Jesus, our newborn sun!

Suddenly, we are no longer talking of a 'stretch' in the evenings because light has found a foothold and will rule undiminished until mid-September finds this twosome back on equal terms in each other's arms.

This sacred moment holds out such hope for all creation as the sunlight grows stronger and brings joy to the land and its inhabitants. When Seamus Heaney writes, 'So long for air to brighten, Time to be dazzled and the heart to lighten,' he could be referring to this time of year – the burden of winter lifted, the planting begun.

Animal Presence

To live slowly we do not need to retire to a monastery or withdraw from the fascinating life around us. The 'slow lane' is about presence not distance. It is about our ability, much underused, to knock at the door of the heart and wait.

I remember a man arriving at a little clinic in Lesotho, Africa, only to find that the nurse, Sr Una, would not return for a few hours. He said he would wait and settled down in a most relaxed way. By contrast, our Western lives seem more and more marked by impatience, irritation, anger and panic.

I visited the Natural History Museum recently. Everything was there: elephant, bat, shark, linnet, lion … but wonderful as it was, something was missing; that is, *animal presence*. No animal heartbeat, no godlike foot was heard, no body was at home!

This can happen to us. It's not easy to come into our own presence, to experience being alive *now*; to *deliberately* look, listen, taste, breathe and smile. People who are 'grounded' have real presence – and they evoke presence in others! They seem to be able to wait when they must and let life be. They can listen in to the whisperings of creation knowing that everything has its voice; that everything speaks of *silent presence*.

'There's slow', writes the poet Lavinia Greenlaw, 'and there's the discovery of slow.'

Five a Day

The Dalai Lama says, 'We have bigger houses but smaller families; more conveniences but less time; more knowledge but less judgment. We've been all the way to the moon and back, but we have trouble crossing the street to meet the new neighbours.'

The problem, he suggests, is that we don't know when we have enough and we trade our hearts for just that little bit more, ending up with 'much in the window, but nothing in the room'.

We need to start nourishing ourselves; befriending nature, reading slowly, lighting a candle, meeting up with friends and enjoying our food; in other words, savouring the lives we have.

When Eddie was diagnosed with terminal cancer, he decided that he would keep a 'thank-you journal'. So every night he would write down five things that he was thankful for. Very soon he had a problem. Which five would he choose? As soon as he began to look at his life in this way there was just so much to be grateful for each day!

'Go into the private room of your heart, close the door and meet your true self.' We may, of course, be afraid of finding nothing there. Still the inner room is where I meet my nearest, most neglected neighbour – myself! In 'Love After Love', Derek Walcott describes that moment when 'with elation, you will greet yourself arriving at your own door, in your own mirror and each will smile at the other's welcome and you will give back your heart to itself'.

Horse Sense

Life isn't an emergency
Richard Carlson

In the film *Speed*, a young cop must prevent a bus's speed from dropping below 50 mph. If he fails a bomb, which has been wired up to the engine, will explode. As a result, red lights must be run, pedestrians scattered, refuelling managed without stopping. As it's Hollywood, a hero or two show up in time to save the lives of the passengers who will never be the same again.

Could it be that we are on a similar bus ride without knowing it? We're warned to keep up to speed. There may even be threats to put a bomb under us and we often live as if we believed that to be so! The message appears to say that the faster we can do something, the better. Soon we cannot live without that power surge, the busyness, the adrenalin rush. To the cartoon farmer leaning over his gate who shouts at the rider galloping past, 'Where are you going in such a hurry?' the reply comes back, 'I don't know, ask the horse.'

When we have lived for too long in the fast lane, it's really hard to slow down. It feels, at first, like living in slow-motion. We find ourselves talking in sentences instead of syllables; walking just for the joy of it as a little voice whispers, 'Not all those who loiter are lost.'

Back on the road we may read those signs which shout at us, SPEED KILLS, and realise that among its victims are leisure, freedom, affection, participation, creativity and prayer. HEED YOUR SPEED, they advise, and ARRIVE ALIVE.

Manners

Faced with a world gone so speedy, you take a risk to live at a walking pace. It's not simply about going slow but about moving in a way that brings your whole being forward.

When we were small, 'to go for a walk' meant a family outing, an excursion. Being treated to an ice cream on the return journey made it special as my father pushed a pram full of tired children up the last stretch. John Masefield's 'Tewkesbury Road' seems so remote to us now: 'It is good to be out on the road, and going one knows not where …' It's also a long time since a man waving a red flag walked ahead of the first motorcar.

In her poem, 'Manners (for a Child of 1918)', Elizabeth Bishop wrote: 'My grandfather said to me as we sat on the wagon seat, "Be sure to remember to always speak to everyone you meet."' Later in the poem she alludes to the unmannerly effect that the new form of transport would have on people's lives; 'When automobiles went by the dust hid the people's faces but we shouted "Good day! Good day! Fine day!" at the top of our voices.'

Our 'hidden' faces as motorists can allow us to be mean and irresponsible and to rage at others. Courtesy restores our human features; the nod of recognition, the salute, and sometimes even a smile (or a double wink from the rear lights!).

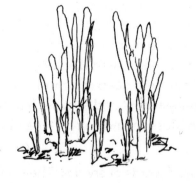

Bookends

'Is Mary there?' a shaky voice enquires and I reply, 'You must have the wrong number.' 'Sorry,' he says, 'sorry about that.' Though our conversation has been brief, I am left wondering, 'Who is Mary?'

Could she be a daughter, home-help, friend? I could imagine him standing in the hallway and checking the number. Was he calling to ask her to collect his pension or to say that he wasn't feeling well. Or perhaps he just needed to hear a familiar voice to reassure him that he was not alone in the world.

In a real conversation there is bodily presence and you don't have to answer immediately. Good conversation allows for a breathing space in which words embroider silence (not simply replace it), like the comforting murmur of parents' voices coming in waves as the children fall off to sleep. It's that good when words are not rushed into being.

When Jesus once approached a woman at a well in Samaria with the request 'give me a drink' it turned out to be a life-changing conversation. They talked about what really mattered to them – relationships and fetching water, life-giving water! Because he spoke and listened from somewhere deep in himself, his words came to her as refreshment and release. She had met the long-awaited Messiah and couldn't wait to tell the whole town.

We use hundreds of words every day. They can bless and affirm or be simply bookends to conversations that never happen.

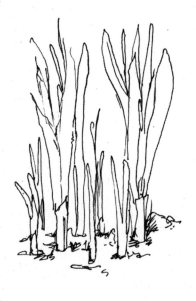

Tell me a Story

In this century, and moment of mania …
tell me a story of deep delight
Robert Penn Warren

Ever since the first glimmer of self-awareness dawned in our ancestors, we have been telling stories to make sense of who we are.

A good story can save us. The best constantly surprise and are often the ones shared at a bus stop, on a bar stool or at bedtime. We cannot live without them.

When we struggle at times with the adventure of our own life story – the angels and demons we meet, times we get lost, accidents, small victories and failures, burdens carried, encounters, death and new life – it's good to think of God as our companion listening in as the narrative unfolds.

And, wonderfully, our stories are set within a larger story of God loving all of us into being. This is our sacred epic of how the universe began from a tiny seed 13.8 billion years ago; how galaxies and stars formed and then our homeplace, Earth, then life in its endless variety and, lately, us, with our love of stories, asking questions and wondering.

As Mary pondered, into our family came her son who listened to our stories and embraced them. When he spoke to us of abundant life we might have been listening to a father telling us about the creation he loves. One hearing is never enough. We hear it always for the first time and with the open-mouthed amazement of children.

A Bit of Real

Some years ago, the American novelist, Paul Auster, invited people to send him stories drawn from their own lives for possible radio broadcast; he received thousands. The stories he looked for were not meant to be literary – just true and short. As you'd expect, they were ordinary as bread, incidents you'd casually share with family and friends – coincidences, journeys, amusing blunders, brushes with death and unexpected joy.

From so much correspondence, one line in particular moved him. It came from a man serving a life sentence for murder whose covering letter ended with the following sentence – 'I was never perfect but I am real.' For Paul Auster, that line summed up so much of what became *True Tales of American Life*; the little moment that is full of significance, the rejected stone that becomes the cornerstone.

A friend of mine once said, playfully, 'the man most suitable for resurrection is a dead man.' He was suggesting that to be 'as good as dead' might not be a bad thing. It might turn out to be the beginning of a story that goes, 'I was never perfect but I am real.' Despite our concern with image, our deepest desire is to be real; to find ourselves each morning with our hands open to receive the day straight from the oven in the east where light rises and farther east, east-er!

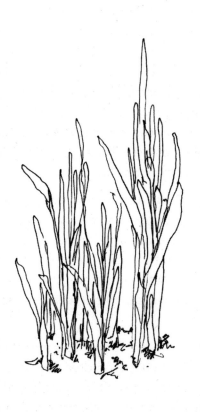

Listening Among the Ruins

Away for the weekend from traffic and the early hammer blows of the building site, the city-dweller claims to hear silence!

It's then I think of boyhood holidays spent with grandparents in Ballyneale, Co. Kilkenny, where my grandfather was creamery manager at Ida. For two weeks every year, the creamery, with its intoxicating smell of milk, was the centre of our world – from the clip-clop of the horse and cart carrying churns in the morning to the quiet that descended each evening. Perhaps, I should say 'ascended' for this rich and textured silence was there all day long under the noise. What arose at six o'clock with the dying machines was birdsong and wind-song and cattle and voices from far away. But other things, too; coded messages from the countryside that entered me without my knowing.

Just last evening I heard about the great grey owl's ability to pinpoint a mouse moving under a cover of snow before it plunges through for the kill. Our ears, by comparison, aren't up to much. The loneliness of a Van Gogh goes unheard. Although there is smoke rising from his chimney, he writes, no one comes in to sit with him by the fire.

Just so, the ruins of the twelfth-century monastery at Monaincha, near Roscrea, go on dreaming of a community living in harmony although the roof is off and the weathered figure on the sandstone cross is barely there! A light breeze rises and towels my face.

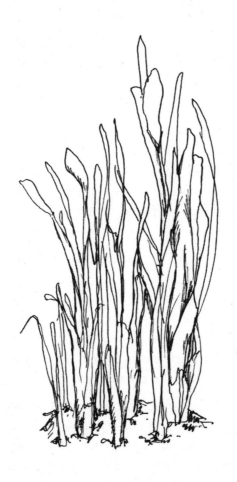

'From Down Where the Hare Sees'

For many years, Kerry Hardie suffered from chronic fatigue. In a poem of hers, entitled 'She Replies to Carmel's Letter' she describes going out for a walk with some friends and finding she has not the energy to continue. She sits down 'like a duck in a puddle' and begins to see things 'from down where the hare sees'. Rather than feel sorry for herself, as she might, sitting in the mud, she remarks, 'Then I would want to praise the ease of low wet things, the song of them, like a child's low drone.'

When a slower pace of life is forced on us by illness, accident or redundancy, the hard questions arise: what value have I now that I can no longer contribute the way I did before? Will people still think well of me? Am I still somebody? And we sigh for those days when we felt in control and had boundless energy.

A young Mary of Mornese (later, foundress of the Salesians Sisters) recovered slowly after a bout of typhoid had taken her to death's door. Her former life of working in the fields was over. In a moment of inspiration, she decided with her best friend, Petronilla, to learn how to sew. It came to her that if every stitch were a stitch of love, her whole being could blossom; she could live in the presence of Love.

Kerry Hardie concludes her poem observing that 'sometimes even sickness is generous and takes you by the hand and sits you beside things you would otherwise have passed over.' Like the importance of a stitch made in love to a world unravelling; or the song of each different thing.

Prayer Plant

I go into our small chapel at dusk and find the plant praying, its leaves raised in salute, perhaps its way of listening. I cannot hope to understand the prayer life of my red herringbone plant, *Maranta tricolor,* and can only surmise. I know for certain it is beautifully and wondrously alive. The red veins in the leaves look painted over a light and a darker green; the undersides are purple red.

Of course the plant is in love with light and knows east from west. I am reminded that it is made with the same loving care as I am. Even when carelessly left thirsty, it seems never to give up on its desire to praise.

Most people never consciously pray with a plant nor do they understand how deeply our fellowship matters; how close we are, how far back we go.

Sometimes when I can't pray myself I can always say to my red herringbone plant, 'Pray for me.' And I know it will not just pray for my need, but pray in my stead; in other words, represent me before the Joy of the universe and make it plain that we are here – both of us – and that our answer is 'Yes'.

In return, I test the soil with a finger and pour a little water for my friend, my John the Baptist sent ahead of us to prepare the way, to arrange the welcome.

Silent Spring

Rachel Carson, in *Silent Spring*, begins in this way. 'There was once a town in the heart of America where all life seemed to live in harmony with its surroundings … with fields of grain and hillsides of orchards where, in spring, white clouds of bloom drifted above the green fields.'

She describes then how some evil spell came to settle on the community with illness and death spreading everywhere. 'There was a strange stillness. The birds, for example – where had they gone? … The feeding stations in the backyards were deserted. The few birds seen anywhere were moribund; they trembled violently and could not fly. It was a spring without voices.'

Written in 1962, her remarkable story is a harrowing account of the destruction caused by the pesticides, insecticides and herbicides sprayed with abandon (with no understanding of how the poison travels step by step from elm leaf to earthworm to robin). Her list of the wild flowers and shrubs under threat as a result reads like a sacred litany –

Azaleas, mountain laurel, blueberries, huckleberries, viburnums, dogwood, bayberry, sweet fern, low shadbush, winterberry, chokeberry and wild plum are dying before the chemical barrage. So are the daisies, black-eyed Susans, Queen Anne's lace, goldenrods, and autumn asters which lend grace and beauty to the landscape

– to each of which we could respond, 'Pray for us.'

Granny-in-Cork

At 4 a.m., I awoke to find that it was National Dawn Chorus Day, the radio bringing the beauty of orchestral birdsong into my room. At once, I opened up and listened for myself. So much energy, such a clamour of voices as the rags of night fell away.

It being also Ascension Day, it seemed that the homecoming of Father and Son was worth chattering about, whistling for, calling out to say that it was all to the good; the homemaking of Father and Son in the heart of creation!

Ciaran O'Driscoll in his book, *A Runner Among Falling Leaves* contrasts two important relationships that marked his whole life. 'I was dying without knowing it. I didn't know a father's love and didn't know that not having a father's love was a kind of dying.' On the other hand, 'Granny-in-Cork fusses happily around, loving the presence of children; imagine, *loving* our presence, and giving us a good feeling about ourselves as she washes the cut on the child's shin and puts on a bandage.'

There is a conversation that goes: 'Will you please listen to me.' 'I am listening.' 'Then why do you not hear me.' As often happens, we hear the words but we don't hear the *person* who is saying them. Like Stevie Smith's sad reflection, 'I was much too far out all my life and not waving but drowning.' The world is full of lonely people who hide behind chirpy words and shaking hands who could do with a 'Granny-in-Cork' in their lives, someone to come home to.

In Memory of Her

'It is the first time in my life that I have been given a cup of tea,' remarked a psychiatric patient to the ministering nurse. Reflecting on her comment, R. D. Laing writes: 'It is not so easy for one person to give another a cup of tea, for a cup of tea could be handed to me without *me* being *given* a cup of tea.' In other words, the action could be a mechanical one in which there is no recognition of *me* in it.

This made me think: is this what it means to give a cup of water 'in my name'? Sometimes, the thought does not count enough! It's *how* the flowers are delivered or the affirmation is given that makes the action a true blessing; being truly nourished as this cup is poured out for *you*.

When Jesus allowed a woman to anoint him with a costly ointment and to kiss his feet tenderly, it was such a deep moment of receiving for him that he wanted that memory of her to become an essential part of his story.

Our life is made happy by the loving details of life rather than by winning the lotto. Perhaps, too, that is why we sometimes confide in a stranger. We share a scrap of our life or a cup of tea without feeling ashamed. We show our hand to another in a single gesture of recognition and acceptance; what R. S. Thomas calls 'peering at eternity through the cracks in each others' hearts' (Caller).

Learning Without Accumulating

On the human adventure we don't know where we are going or what happens next. But we park our doubt and pretend that everything is under control. For the philosopher-sage, Krishnamurti, being able to humbly say 'I don't know' is to be happily in 'a state of learning without accumulating'!

In our insecurity we look to the 'professionals', someone in authority to tell us what to do. But part of being human is to live and move with the big questions: Why are we here? Who are these other creatures? How should we live?

Not everyone wants to hear this. It seems to undermine the flimsy optimism of the times. 'Let's play the latest video game of national security,' we say, until the next climate event all but washes us away. Uncertainty, however, is the artist's friend; where there is risk, there is possibility and a time to play and explore …

'The ragpicker worked in silence and never looked at anything that was whole.' When he found anything perfect it made him sad; what could you do with it? His imagination flared, however, when he found things useless and broken – they could be transformed … 'a twisted piece of pipe. Wonderful, this basket without a handle … Wonderful, a box without a key. Wonderful, half a dress, the ribbon off a hat, a fan with a feather missing. Wonderful' (*Ragtime*, Anaïs Nin).

When Bad Things Happen

It's all very well to talk about laughing and singing your way through life but for many people it can sound like so much cheap talk. And what do you say to victims of typhoon, famine, war?

There are money matters, health matters, troubles of all kinds. Still, people with heavy burdens of care, debt or immobility can surprise you with a burst of faith and a joy in being alive. Like Brian who found himself paralysed following a tractor accident. During twenty-three years of incapacity and acceptance (and being completely cared for), he grew in life-giving presence, retaining his sense of fun and a love for the cows and donkeys in his care.

In a shaky hand, Wendy wrote these words the week before she died. 'Every day I am reminded of how frail the human body is – decay, disease, injury, illness – so what is left to do? – become fearful, angry, confused? Rather, she concludes, 'Trust in God and a purpose in all of this and a handing over and complete surrender to Him is the only way for me to go.'

Make a skylight, suggests Rumi, the great Sufi mystic, for 'the house without a window is hell'. Open the window of your soul so that 'the rain of divine grace and the light can fall on you'. As happens on the stroke of illness or misfortune when a window opens between hearts and one recognises a friend.

A Question of Size

Size is no measure of complexity
Linnaeus

When extended to all creatures, Jesus' teaching that 'every hair on your head has been counted', reminds us that every whisker, thorn, or feather has its function and is part of an exquisite design in which the creator delights!

Fear of other creatures, however, prevents us from knowing them. 'I kill it because I have been told to,' writes Jo Shapcott in her poem 'Scorpion', 'I kill it by slapping my shoe against the wall … I kill it to feel sure I will live … I kill it because I do not understand it. I kill it without looking at it … I kill it because it will not speak to me.'

I know the feeling, having scoured white walls in a Maltese night for the mosquito who sips my blood. In my moment of panic, her beauty and the majesty of her emergence escapes me. I leave blood behind, hers and mine!

Human history says: *homo homini lupus*; we fear the 'wolf' in each other. And fear can drive us to behave abominably. With fear in our eyes we don't see clearly any more; something well expressed as 'your enemy's tears are only water'. Without empathy we see 'only water'; his are not real tears – not like ours!

A loving eye, on the other hand, takes a longer and a closer look; allows for the beauty in difference and celebrates it. When God speaks in his native tongue, the 'words' he utters are *scorpion, swallow, worm!*

Neighbours

Driving along, I notice a dead body by the roadside. No one has stopped. Could it be that no one has noticed. True, it doesn't look like anyone we know wrapped up in a fur coat but it has the signs of a hit and run.

The adult badger did not go home last night. Impossible to think that he was not missed. Convenient to say that badgers spread disease and don't feel like we do. Of course, we could equally say that we don't feel like they do.

In my passing glance he looked thrown there without a second thought as though life did not once flow as knowingly through his whole being as through ours. It occurred to me that few tears, if any, would be shed for a neighbour who lived locally, had raised a family, learnt to survive with a unique intelligence, praised God in his own way. Yet no Good Samaritan might be expected to stop to check his wounds or say a prayer. The Road Safety Authority would not be informed.

At the time of his treaty with the European settlers in 1854, Chief Seattle of the Squamish tribe is reported to have said that when the last animals will have perished humans would die of loneliness. Day by day, our fellow creatures are dying out, often due to the demands of human 'progress'. Can we survive this soul loss?

Soil Mates

We must uncentre our minds from ourselves
Robinson Jeffers

Long before we are soul mates with anyone, we are soil mates with everything! We come from the same source. Earth is our mother, the womb of all life. Of course we are conditioned to think of ourselves as superior to everything else and more favoured by God! However, our deepest being, according to the scriptures, is to be 'Adam' (earthling), whose name comes from 'Adamah', the Hebrew word for earth. The Jewish poet, Samuel Menashe, has great fun with this association when he writes, 'I am the man whose name is mud'!

It's a moment of grace when this truth dawns on us, namely, that we are cousins with everything, part of a family in which we are different but not separate. We can never be lonely again! The miracle is that in the endless variety of all creatures we discover who we really are and catch glimpses of the 'goodness' of the one we call God.

These days I am watching a leaf of my prayer plant opening. It seems that nothing is happening yet each morning I am surprised at how busy the plant has been. It's obvious we have different ways of doing time! After some days, the new leaf, which first appeared as a tightly rolled up scroll, holds out its hand and says, 'Read me.' And I have to admit I don't know how.

'Teach me,' I reply.

Cherry Blossom, Heywood

I went out on a spring day with my new camera. It had a zoom lens and I was excited about snapping the flowers close-up. I placed myself beside the cherry tree and fixed my camera eye on a branch heady with blossom. I noticed, however, that just as I was about to click and take my picture, the branch moved in a light wind. It bowed and swayed, dipped and rose, or just trembled.

I stood there waiting for it to be still, with a hint of impatience, as if the tree should obey me, just because I happened to come along at one moment in its long life. Where had I been all the winter when it was contemplating birth and death and feeling its way in hope? And where would I be when the last shower of confetti would drift away?

It was so arrogant when I thought about it, to chide the cherry for being ecstatic in May when at last it could express its inner life as a heartbreaking mass of pink petals. 'Stay still and behave,' I was insisting, wishing to control the threshing branches in their alleluias, but they were having none of it.

Is this how we live, how we share a common acre with the plants and animals – lording it over them, ungrateful for their wise company, as we continue our anxious debate about who is the greatest? Sadly, it's quite possible to spend our un-whole lives trying to be something that we are not, while before us the cherry blossom, silent as God-speech, invites us to dance.

Summer

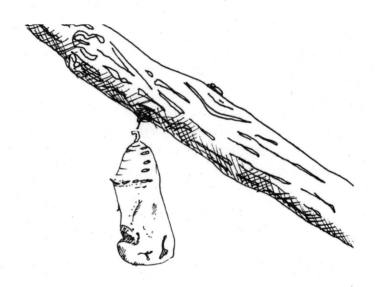

Brother Sun

Often in June I find myself on the west coast of Donegal looking out at sunsets and noting how the last flicker can stretch past midnight. Summer with its memories and longing is upon us. Near Kincasslagh I notice the children adding to the growing mound that will be a bonfire on St John's Eve, a feast that coincides with the longest day of the year – the summer solstice.

We know that earlier communities would have lit their fires as a way of calling on the sun at its highest point to make their crops fertile. Recent accounts describe a festival with music, singing, games, dancing and leaping through the flames while torches of firelight were held aloft and carried through the fields for protection. Some brought home an ember for their own hearth or a shovelful of red hot sods as foundation for a new house. Even the ashes had curative powers and were spread on the land as a blessing.

Thinking about these things, brings us down to earth and causes us to wonder. What kind of God uses the elements manufactured in the core of a star then scattered abroad in a supernova explosion to make life and creates in timescales beside which our life span is no more than the single pulse of a firefly?

Making these connections is to celebrate that we are part of a dazzling communion; that the providential tilt of the Earth allows us to have seasons; that our remote origins are overlaid with the blessing, 'You are my beloved on whom my favour rests.'

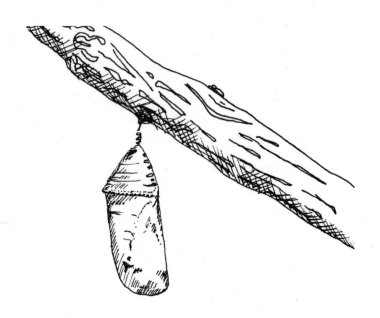

Leaf Miner

The first time was on my way home from school. As I turned off from Drimnagh Road a glance to my left saw a boy rolling down the incline outside Browne's Bookies. A bus had knocked him over. The crowd gathered and the ambulance was on its way.

I have come across accidents since and have seen a man lying dead in the middle of the road. I have also seen the badger, cat, fox, dog, rat, crow, hedgehog with their guts showing. But we get used to the litter of death and hardly notice the black feathers stuck to the tar.

I visited John one July and watched as he untangled a hollyhock which was being strangled by bindweed and pulled to the ground. We had time, so we sat and inspected the lichen on the pavement and watched the mites scurrying around looking for some body to take them further. Going inside I peered into the microscope at a bramble leaf full of scribbles (signs of the progress of the leaf-miner *stigmella splendidissimella*) and another world unfolded beyond my feeble sight.

The road less travelled may turn out to be the best way to go. After a while one tires of the motorway and begins to long for the secondary road where the heart is not beating quite so fast. Deep down something in us is saying 'slow down' and at the same time we are speeding up. We're funny old beings and just as innocent as the night animal who wanders onto a highway or the boy dashing across the street with a packet of crisps in his hand.

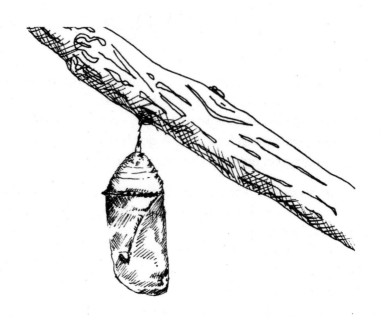

Swings

Of all the activities in the playground, nothing excites like the swings. There must be something in our genes that makes us delight in soaring up from the ground, backwards and forwards. A good push and away we go, holding on tight and letting go inside.

In his poem 'The Swing', Seamus Heaney describes the homemade swing set up in their shed where a rope reached down and was fitted with an old, lopsided sack to form the seat. To his grown-up child's eye it hung like 'a lure let down to tempt the soul to rise'. He talks about his overworked mother and remembers how she sat there once to please the children, 'just tempted by it for a moment only'.

Isn't that a bit like us? Tired out but 'tempted' to let go. Then the moment passes, the magic turns ordinary though we can still feel the exhilaration in our bodies as we pass a playground and see the children pushing off like the children we once were. It must count as one of the saddest things when we lose our sense of wonder. It takes a clown sometimes or a child to remind us who we really are as she sails into the sky out of her depth.

Indonesian Rainstick

From childhood, our eyes are drawn to those who win – gold, silver and bronze – and not to the others full of panting as they stumble across the finish line. *O, the ease of a walking pace and no more effort!*

Meanwhile the winner draped in a national flag welcomes the sniping cameras as she suddenly finds herself famous, everybody's darling. This is victory! This is paradise!

Behind her the also-rans slope off down the tunnel back to the life they knew. Who sees them? Maybe they remind us of ourselves. And we wouldn't miss the fantasy of winning for anything. Tears on a podium are more eloquent than the stifled tears of the one who comes last.

Watching the Olympics reminds me of how Jesus seized on the word 'last' and turned it upside down. There is another way of seeing, he said, where there is no distinction between first and last. Not in the future but right now.

Consider the rainstick, a length of hollow bamboo full of dried seeds. It leans silently against the wall until you upend it and then you hear a shushing sound like water flowing through. Listen. What you thought ordinary is suddenly magical. It's just a matter of turning it upside down in a game where nobody wins and no one loses!

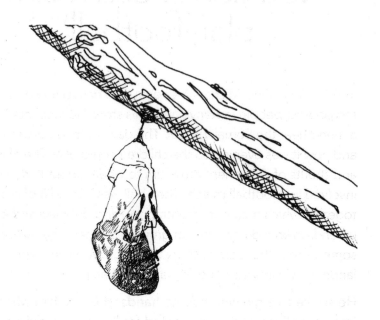

'You don't need feet to play football'

In *All Will Be Well*, Michael Meegan, who has spent years among the poorest people in Kenya, tells this story. He recounts visiting a friend near the Somali border. The day had been extremely hot and now it was evening so the children could play. Their laughter and shouts of enjoyment drew him to where about thirty were involved in a football match. Their ball was a bundle of rags tied together which their bare feet trapped and dribbled and kicked up and down a dusty patch of ground. Suddenly he realised that some were without arms, some without feet. Most were landmine victims from the Somali Civil War.

He spoke to a girl who had no hands who told him where the imaginary lines were and giggled for he was standing on the pitch! A young teenage boy arrived in a cloud of dust beside him and smiled. His legs had been blown off beneath the knees. He told of what position he was playing and who his favourite players were. Mike asked him was it harder to play football now than before. Just before charging back into the game he said, with that smile of incomprehension, 'You don't need feet to play football.' Then he vanished up the line heading the ball.

We could learn. We have feet but find it hard to play. We have arms but are often afraid to reach out. We have smiles that are unused; laughter that is seldom drawn from the well. If we don't need feet to play football, then maybe we don't need 'a voice' to sing! It seems that it's not about ability but about heart. If you really want to live, this young boy says, then take a deep breath, step across the imaginary line of fear, and join in.

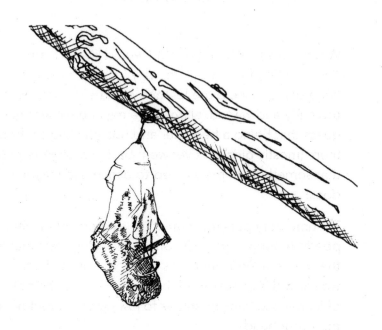

Dancer

When I was twelve, I thought I would like to learn Irish dancing. So after school one day I found my way to a large garage where the lessons were held. I was an hour too early and waited, all the time my interest waning. I guess that being a beginner and not knowing anybody there (mostly girls), I never went back. I recognise now that something in me wanted to dance and maybe still does.

That memory puts me in mind of a comment on Yeats' poem 'Among School Children' which suggests that for the poet real education was all about dance; 'how can we know the dancer from the dance?' I love the notion of learning as movement, as following your heart no less than your head!

On Sean McDermott Street I often see the infants on their way from school stepping up so they can walk along the two-foot-high wall outside the Church. A parent's steadying hand is usually waved away! Instinctively, they recognise a challenge even at this age and want to show just how grown up they are.

It takes us much longer to realise that our dancing hearts and feet are *being danced* into life by the Creator whose nature is Dance! Until that awakening, we can do our own dodge and shuffle, keeping our balance, learning poise. It is a blessing the day we decide to let go and allow ourselves *be danced* to the (never-ending) end of Love.

Bundoran

I stood near the edge of the sea in August of a poor summer. It was evening but the shrieks of fear and excitement from the small bodies in the water were saying that weather didn't matter. The holiday town was buzzing. The Big Wheel turned its circle of lights while the young braves stepped on-board 'Oblivion' to undergo an ordeal that would turn them upside down and inside out.

There is something simple and enduring about making that annual pilgrimage. You do it for the children and for your own childhood and go to where sand and wave greet each other like long-lost friends.

It's there you will find candy floss and sand in the sandwiches; children in need of a parent's comforting; teenagers finding themselves in love; adults pulled out of adulthood and carrying home a shell; older folk sitting out in the fresh air, watching a dark cloud rolling in.

Isaiah could not have put it better, 'Come to the water all you who are thirsty; though you have no money come.' He was thinking of the Holiday-Giver who offers us the break we can all afford; the chance to lay down our burdens in a restful moment and know His presence in our need.

And then come two reminders. Firstly, there is Ellen, at two years, who refuses to pass by a puddle without making a splash. She knows a little ocean when she sees one.

Secondly, months later, rummaging in a drawer, you come across a postcard from some sunny place and know that you were remembered and missed, even briefly, in that familiar way: 'Wish you were here'.

Sea Campion

The blackbird goes on singing his song of the present moment. It's not his fault that I am listening to other voices. If I could really listen to his tune I would hear myself. I would hear myself listening!

*

This man listens to music to make the loss of his wife bearable. This woman cannot bear music in the house since her husband died. On a June evening the cuckoo announces the ache and joy of being alive.

*

'So that's sea campion,' I say and he replies, 'It's always been there. Maybe you didn't know what to look for.' We tramp around much of the time, our eyes drawn inwards to our human concerns. But whoever made us also made the sea campion and its friend the sea pink.

*

I observe a grandfather taking his grandson down to the beach. The little boy is busy asking questions about this and that, seeing it all for the first time, bending down to a flower or insect. Most likely he will forget such moments until he is bringing his own children to the beach and fumbling for answers.

*

The natural world speaks in a thousand voices. We are part of that chorus praising the One who can speak to us in the form of sea campion or an inquisitive child.

Herb Robert

'What are you doing here on Sean McDermott Street?' I say to herb robert, surprised to find that small face peering through the railings fronting Joe Costelloe's clinic. Not too many will notice him on their way in to see Joe with one problem or another – rent arrears, anti-social activities, or getting a window put in. Of course herb robert is not paying rent and appears quite happy to live in the full force of weather.

Suddenly we seem so fragile beside *geranium robertianum* who has found such a perfect niche in which to unfold. We know the phrase, 'consider the lilies' and we could add, 'consider herb robert' who is also telling us something we find hard to accept, namely, that we share a Father who provides for us.

So we make our way past this little fellow lying by the gate as another image comes to mind of the homeless, wasted figure of Lazarus lying outside the house of Dives. Maybe poor people and wild flowers have this in common – they are often overlooked.

In contrast, the wreaths that accompany a coffin appear extravagant. Would a flower from a garden or from a roadside in June not say more of our frailty and raise our hope in the One whose eyes search for us even when the light has gone out.

The Man on the Corner

The man who stands for hours on the corner talking to himself is one of us. It's like he is arguing with himself (or someone else) or working things out in public as he paces up and down or moves in circles as his imaginary opponent drifts this way or that. Were we to stop, he would remind us of our own inner chatter, the endless debate, our dilemma: 'What have we done? What can we do now?'

There is a way of crying for ourselves, for our not being whole and wise and generous, which is not self-pity. As when we grieve for the loved one who has died and cry for ourselves at the same time, a deep agonising prayer of loss for what we are not and can never be in our own eyes. It is a cry for light in the dark, for mother to come and chase the nightmare away; a longing to see the face of love, to be held as good, to be home again.

In Costa, over coffee, David and I talk of how they go together, grief and regret, and how we might dare to look at our old failures, the time we have wasted, opportunities declined. And parents? 'They still keep loving us,' I say, and it seems right to believe it and to believe their love still reaches us over time like an afterglow from their first kiss.

Three Little Pigs

We are often reminded that we live in a flimsy house built of thoughts, which is not the kind of place you'd choose to spend your whole life! What with the shifting, drifting nature of thinking, it's hard to get a foothold or feel at home.

In a house made of thoughts, there are no windows, the bricks are porous, the roof forever in a state of repair as one image replaces another. Which reminds me of the three little pigs building their house of straw. And how the wolf came: 'He huffed and he puffed and he blew the house down.'

Despite ourselves, we can live a lifetime in our prison-house of thoughts – of grudges, fears, worries, regrets – while waiting for life to kick in. When we mistake our thoughts for the real thing, we just go on rebuilding with the same old material – unlike the little pigs!

That is until we wake up and see through our paper-thin walls, open the door and step outside to a real world awaiting our precious attention.

Breathe.

It's summer. Look at a bush full of bees on a nectar trip, hear a bird speaking out and feel the breeze on your face. The world is addressing you as friend. Come out to play, it says. Wise up, will you.

Breathe.

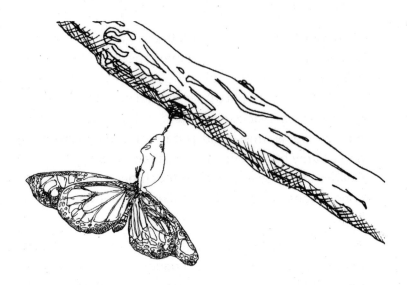

Just Lingering

Even though I grew up along the seam where Crumlin meets Walkinstown, my first memories are of my father digging in the garden, planting potatoes, cabbage, onions, beetroot, rhubarb and lettuce. We had gooseberries, blackcurrants and strawberries. There I met my first worms, snails and beetles, heard birdsong and put my hands into clay like the original potter. Children instinctively want to touch base, to make connections, to splash in puddles. We are gardeners at heart.

To live life to its fullest is to live in awareness that all is one: that God is in all – from dandelion to human to the teeming life in a spoonful of earth. It is a mystical way open to everyone! Of course it will take the discipline of love to give time each day to simply be and to 'let be'; to utter praise by just being still and letting the world come to us.

In Mary Oliver's poem 'The Place I Want to Get Back To' she describes an encounter she had while sitting quietly in the pinewoods one morning before dawn as two deer approached her nervously:

> and then one of them leaned forward
> and nuzzled my hand, and what can my life
> bring to me that could exceed
> that brief moment.

That was twenty years ago and still she goes to the same woods, 'not waiting exactly, just lingering'. She has named her house *Gratitude*.

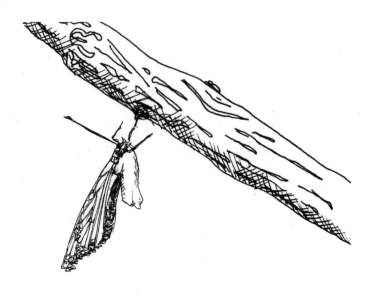

Corncrake and Cuckoo

That summer I was lucky. I heard the corncrake and the cuckoo, two voices less and less common in Ireland. On Tory Island, the corncrake's *crek-crek, crek-crek*, though not melodious, was especially welcome as a voice I hadn't heard for years. The islanders have done well in offering sanctuary to this ground-nesting bird who was once a full citizen of our hay fields.

Just as the Creator expresses himself through all of the different beings, so a light of divine presence goes out when a species becomes extinct. When a unique song note is silenced it may not seem to matter but it does; creatures who have travelled the bumpy road of evolution with us are truly neighbours. Their going diminishes us.

Once we faced east to greet our rising Sun, 'the light of the world', but that tradition is no longer upheld. Having lost a sense of our whereabouts, we are less likely to recognise that the cosmos is praying with us; that corncrake and cuckoo are speaking of Christ in their acclamation of praise!

We are misled when we think it a good thing to withdraw from creation in order to praise God. Rather, it is comforting to know that we are not alone when we pray. The birds have well finished matins by the time we get up and step outside!

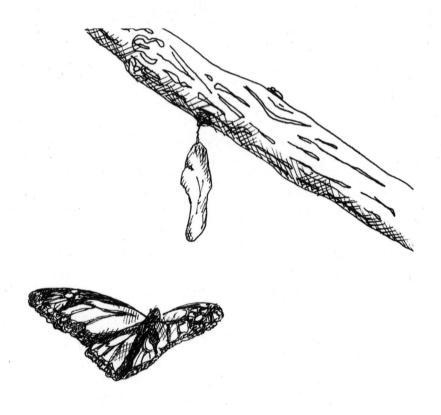

The Singing Bird

Of a summer's morning Rose Mooney would burst into song. She had a good voice and wasn't ashamed to let it rip. She sang in the kitchen with the back door open, sang while hanging out the washing, sang to announce herself despite what neighbours might say.

It's clear that when we sing we do something playful with our breath and with our speech, releasing those happy airs in the brain. And it's contagious. How often do you find someone humming a tune he or she has heard earlier but can't quite remember from where? There is a melody of love that searches the world for someone to sing and pass it on.

In a Cistercian or Benedictine monastery, you will find that the monks and sisters chant the praise of God seven times a day. It is not a performance and not everyone can keep in tune but it is prayer and an antidote to the way we can misuse our voice to condemn, to silence or deceive.

I remember a boy whose party piece was 'The Singing Bird' before self-consciousness caused him to go dumb. (Now he needs a few pints to get started!) It struck me then how a song will follow a person all his life:

> the boy soprano
> who sang 'The Singing Bird' now
> whistles on Death Row.

There is still a child in the criminal; that whistle was once his song.

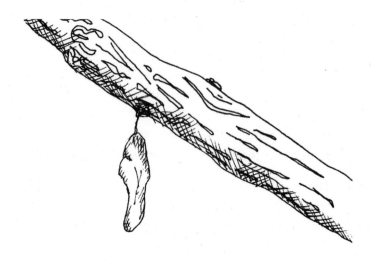

Habiba

There is something instinctive about taking off your shoes by the sea. Has it to do with origins or memories of childhood? Either way, there's nothing like the scratch of warm sand between your toes and the chance to remember that your first steps were taken barefoot.

This evening, a phrase of Hopkins is recalled, 'nor can foot feel being shod', as we ease our way into the shallows of the Atlantic. We paddle along and soon the first shock of cold water feels more and more like refreshment. We begin to appreciate the instruction to Moses from the burning bush, 'Take off your shoes for the ground you walk upon is holy.'

Heavy drops pick us out but with nowhere to shelter we decide not to run. Maybe it's good to be caught out at times and to welcome rain!

In a holding area for immigrants in Frankfurt airport, Habiba, an African child, plays outside in the yard under a small square of sky. She is dancing barefoot in a shower of hail, trying to catch the white beads she has never seen before, to pick them up and taste them. For a moment or two those seeking entry are delighted by her sense of wonder and play; they even forget that the ground beneath them is virtual space – officially it does not exist! Her mother's request for the two of them to enter the country will be processed in due course and then turned down.

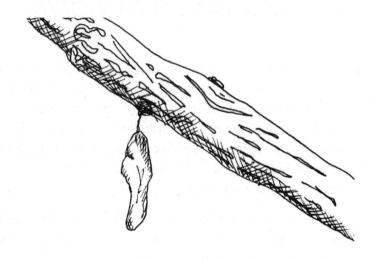

Sharing a Shadow

In the Persian language, the word for neighbour means 'someone who shares your shadow'. It is a marvellous image and recalls the Irish, *is ar scáth a chéile a mhaireann na daoine* – 'people live in each other's shadow'. Despite its negative connotation since Carl Jung linked it to the unconscious side of our lives, the reality is such a magical thing.

A shadow walks beside you, stops when you stop and matches your every move. And remember the first time someone made shadowy shapes on a wall for you!

This morning sunlight shines in behind me and I can see my outline as a giant fallen on the floor. I get down on my knees and view the dome of my head with two ledges on either side – handles or primitive ears!

'Hello shadow,' I say, because it's years since we had a word. I look again at that baby head, the image like an ultra scan of the bald man I later became. This is promise foretold, the gift of myself in embryo. You begin as a shadow but grow up to be much more solid than that.

Still that shadow is the dancing part of you that can elongate or climb walls or change shape effortlessly though the light is not always positioned to see it. I turn round and give the thumbs up to the sun. It's time to hang out again with my other half, then go sit in my neighbour's shadow and mingle.

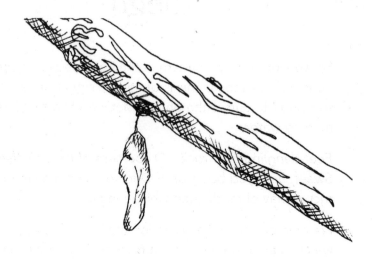

Elegy

So we stopped by a stream in the Poisoned Glen and removed our shoes. This is of cosmic significance, I said, showing off; ours is the only planet we know that has running water.

Feet dangling over rocks, O coolness of the universe! Sweet, honeyed bog water! Our words no match for the tricksy play of modulated whisperings.

I ramble on but when I mention the word 'heaven', I watch in amazement a tear tumble from your eye and slide down your cheek. Maybe 'water' is the better word for loss, I say to myself, and imagine that this is the shape Michael has assumed for now to greet us, the same element he was once baptised into: 'Water you are and to water you will return.'

So whose tear is it that fell from your eye? Could it be his? And your eye now become his lookout? Just so, the whole universe which has poured itself into fashioning us is also transformed into a tear and in some sense cries in us. Ours the eye then, through which the universe marvels at its own beauty and mystery. We are sacraments of the earth! The earth in human form!

Surrender to being here and not here. Dip your feet in deeper. Let them be anointed for a fuller life; feeling silky and cared-for now inside shoes, sleepy and ready for bed.

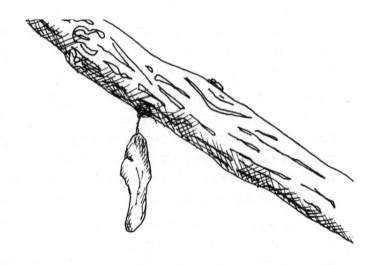

A Taster

It seems a long time since I heard someone describe a delightful experience as 'heavenly', although people of a certain age will still say so.

To them it seems natural to recognise a moment, a summer's day, for instance, as a taster of future bliss, of being finally at home in oneself. They imagine that this could be Eden and they the first humans to feast their senses on the beauty of the earth as lovers, parents, friends; their joy an echo of God's own joy in creation.

Because we bear the sharp edge of cold weather much of the year, the sudden warmth of sun across our shoulders can call up the word, 'heaven', with a sense of gratitude that lifts our whole body.

And haven, that sister-word, too. For we long to place our feet on the earth and know it as home. Such heaven-haven moments affirm our shared life as good over and over and confirm again the promise that love is our origin and end, what we cling to for dear life.

Of course the gift of this moment of ecstasy, of epiphany, this divine reassurance that all is well doesn't last. These moments are meant to steady us for the time when the angel has gone, the kiss of betrayal is felt and we draw a last breath. We have watched others cross that threshold; later we will cross it ourselves, hopefully with a memory of 'heaven' to sustain us, to give us wings.

Yesterday, Isabel sent me a line she translated from Arabic, 'God is beautiful and likes beauty.'

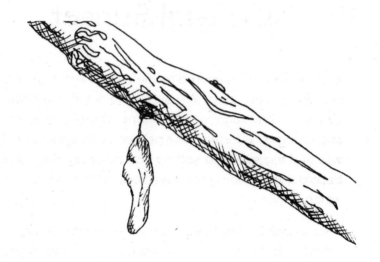

Coastal Sunset

In June, four of us walked to the pier to watch the sun set off the west coast. We became quiet as the bright ball went down against a backdrop of pinks, mauves and oranges. We stood like people at an apparition. It was as if the sun were setting just for us and we, by its bedside, responding to its last request for that day to watch awhile.

Back in Dublin, I notice a little restaurant/takeaway called 'Gobble and Go'. The contrast 'as far as the east is from the west' couldn't have been greater. Eating against the clock has to be like taking a shortcut through a flowerbed where you don't notice whose dreams, time, handiwork you are trampling on.

It's different when it's shared. Then it's about friendship, family, conversation and moments of satisfying silence. The expression 'I'm going for a bite' may fit the gobbler better than the couple who approach their beans on toast as a small feast. Love and food go hand in hand.

It may be twelve months before I see another coastal sunset in all its glory but I am grateful for the reminder to slow down and maybe count to ten before diving into a favourite dish; just long enough to thank the food and the food-giver, those who prepared it and whoever spread the tablecloth with its invisible stars.

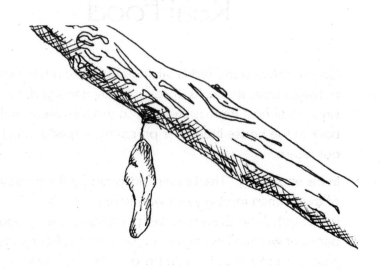

Real Food

On our forest walk, Ted is talking about the relationship between trees and soils. If soil is badly damaged, he says, it's almost impossible for it to recover. Meanwhile back in the house Noreen is preparing a special meal for our return.

In his engraving, 'The Leaven' (inspired by the parable of the woman mixing yeast with flour until it is leavened), John Everett Millais presents us with a poor barefoot woman leaning over a large table; her hands placed on the dough could be kneading or blessing. From around her waist a piece of cloth billows, like the loincloth arranged around the figure of Jesus in depictions of the crucifixion. To her right, a pale-faced girl holds up a loaf of bread for us to see.

The Slow Food movement began in Italy in 1986 as a response to our way of treating food as a commodity – *something* bought in a shop or takeaway with no obvious connection to earth or animal. In contrast, to eat 'slowly' directs us towards food that is locally produced and takes account of its journey from seed to soil, from field to table.

In the background I can hear Ethna insisting that to prepare food in a kitchen is to preside at a liturgy! With the worktable her altar, she, too, reminds us of what the kingdom of heaven is like.

Back home, Ted pours the wine, Noreen lifts the lid. We inhale and say thanks.

Autumn

Earth's Child-Face

Today we celebrate the autumn equinox and these twin mysteries of our existence – darkness and light. The equinox is a sign to us like the star was to the Magi as they traced their way to the cave of the infant king. It suggests that by stalling in September, we, too, can make a similar journey through the natural world to find out more about who we are. Even our language allows that we are creatures of weather – a little weather-beaten, often finding ourselves in the dark yet cheered when we see the light and understanding dawns!

Today we praise day and night in equal measure, each with its paradox – the day with its source in darkness, the dark nurturing seeds of light. The autumn equinox is a slow dance of seeming opposites, light pairing off with shadow and finding completeness. It reminds us of our own deep desire to commune; to be in the dark and to welcome the light, to be in the light and to value the dark as we step out in the awareness of earth's child-face held in the gaze of the sun.

In this season we find ourselves again with that 'oh' and 'ah' on our lips. They are words of affirmation that this is where we live, our strange yet familiar home. We bow our heads to the One we have come to know in the mingling of darkness and light.

Begonias on Sean McDermott Street

This year our hanging baskets were empty. We had forgotten to replant, so it was amazing then that late in August a gorgeous yellow flower should raise itself up and peer over the edge; with every day a deeper yellow, more petticoat, more eye-catching detail.

Explanations fall short. How did it get there? Was it a dormant bulb from last year or a blow-in from a neighbour's garden? Despite our lack of effort, our house is suddenly graced as we feel ourselves chosen, for no obvious reason, to host this beauty.

So what about all this talk of success being 99% perspiration and 1% inspiration? Maybe away from the track and field there is a more gentle logic to be found where only 1% perspiration is required and 99% appreciation!

Many years ago I teased Anna Mary, a Franciscan sister, with the adage that 'God helps those who help themselves' to be immediately put in my place by her reply that 'God helps those rather who are not able to help themselves'. I remember her correction still. To our capitalist minds, God is an entrepreneur who expects a good return on his investment; for Jesus, God is the father who goes on loving his wayward child!

A flower blooms where none was expected. So someone at our door will raise her eyes to this bright welcome and imagine a party where the guests wear something yellow and sip a glass of champagne.

Let us Stop
to Admire an Apple

'Let it lie in the palm of your hand. Close your fingers slowly about it. Put it against your cheek and inhale its fragrance ... for it holds the essence of the year and is in itself a thing of exquisite beauty.'

So writes Liberty Hyde Bailey in *The Holy Earth: Toward a New Environmental Ethic*. Even in 1915 he was worried that humans were losing touch with the earth and its produce, receiving the world, as it were, second-hand.

Today it all sounds a bit nostalgic like his longing to get back to 'a good munch of real apples under a tree or by the fireside'. But if we extend his appreciation of a 'good keeper' to an appreciation of the earth as our 'good keeper', we see how 'we cannot afford to lose this note from our lives'.

Often the best way to love the earth is to begin with an apple or a potato and the miracle of how this marvellous thing was born in your garden soil. Let us have an apple day or an apple sabbath to express our gratitude, Bailey exhorts, for 'we are an apple-growing people'.

Furthermore, a deeper understanding of the earth becomes possible when we take our faith outdoors and greet the God of creation first hand! Then let the first reading be, 'let us stop to admire an apple'. And the words *crop* and *harvest*, *seed* and *season* be a holy communion in our mouths.

Hare and Tortoise

Thirteen-year-old Naoki Higashida tells this story:

Having lost the earlier contest, Hare demands a rematch. Tortoise, as reigning champion, eventually concedes to Hare's request. The animals gather. At the gun, Hare streaks away. Tortoise, pumped up with adrenalin, trips over something and ends up on his back. The animals carry him home. Later, when Hare crosses the line, punching the air, there is nobody there to cheer.

In *The Reason I Jump*, Naoki allows us access to the hypersensitive world of someone considered slow and uncommunicative. With remarkable insight, he gives us a glimpse into autism with its fears and uncertainties. Time, for example, he says, is 'as difficult for us to grasp as picturing a country we've never been to … exactly what the next moment has in store for us never stops being a big, big worry.'

No wonder he writes of his longing to go back to a 'distant, distant watery past' before our ancestors crawled onto dry land and discovered time.

Even when ignored or pushed away, he finds solace and friendship in nature from whom 'we receive a sort of permission to be alive in this world and our entire bodies get recharged … Nature will always give us a great big hug here in our hearts'. Just by looking at nature, he says, he can feel swallowed up into it, a sensation so amazing 'I forget that I'm a human being and one with special needs as well'.

And the black crow looked no less perfect against the deep blue than the white dove.

What News?

The day I heard, 'Our life like a bird has escaped from the snare of the fowler,' I thought of how we can all find ourselves at times flapping about helplessly, held fast by one bad memory, one idea, a particular addiction, circling about ourselves and going nowhere.

The image of a bird escaping the snare evokes in us the joy of being alive and the exhilaration of a big sky and a playful wind. Psalm 124 implies that someone has broken the snare for us. Love has set us free!

The poet R. S. Thomas puts it well when he observes that 'we cover the ground faster but what news do we bring?' Is it news of being free, of having second and third chances, of encouragement to spread our wings and rise above our fears? In a world where our desires are sometimes as small as the product we are persuaded to buy, we can starve for a bit of good news.

There are ways of being great that may not be newsworthy; as when we reach out and undo the snare for each other. This graceful gesture might be as simple as pointing out a patch of blue in a cloudy sky, or giving a hug instead of advice. Either way, it seems to say, 'Haven't you noticed, the snare is broken … No, silly, you don't need wings. Come on. Let's fly.'

At the Alliance Française

There's no such thing as a miserable day
Michael Moran

O, the freedom of 'nothing matters that much'! The sense of a burden lifted from your shoulders as the strong hands of an imaginary sun press deeply down to the point of stress. Now there's time for another coffee and a longer conversation.

In the car park I stop for a few minutes in the after-drizzle of a heavy shower and watch the water pouring through the broken gutter and squirting from the pierced downpipe while the main course gushes into a flooded drain clogged with weeds. 'Many things are urgent', I recall, 'but how many are important?'

Later, in the café, I meet Philip and we make plans to return to French because it's September and if we don't do something another term will pass us by. So we resolve to put into practice all the wisdom of the ages and to observe the '7 Laws of Happiness' (or were they '7 Steps' to be followed? Better not get stuck on a detail when we're that close to a decision!).

'Just breathe,' I offer, having heard that somewhere, 'that's where it's all supposed to start.' And then we return to normal conversation and all is well with the world. And we're coming around to see that the things that matter are few enough – collect Jeanne Marie from school, buy some flowers for Sandra and uncork that bottle you've been keeping for a rainy day!

'Have you Caught Anything?'

The Drowes pulsed like a living thing, its waters dark and sinewy. It was a good fishing river, judging by the number of cars and their county registrations. Scattered along its banks were the fishermen, in waders, casting. With a flick of the wrist, a line sang through the air, and dropped halfway across. Occasionally, a salmon heading upstream would make a splash as he leaped for a fly. In that serene setting, few words, if any, were said. The men (mostly) were happy just being there, in tune with the river. They moved like people in a trance, following some inner prompting; appeared as monks silently pursuing an ordinary task for its hidden meaning.

I was impressed and a little envious. And yet I had seen that attention before in a person gardening, in a farmer's eyes, in a woman in a clothes shop feeling the fabric, in a child at play, in the shake of hands lighting a candle.

These are the moments we lose our self-consciousness and forget the many 'shoulds' and 'oughts' that have accumulated over years. It's as if our whole being (mind and heart) were moving in the same direction; as if *success* and *failure* didn't exist – as if that distinction had never been made.

Such moments of unfolding (or in-folding) are outside time as when you notice that the pot plant you are tending is attending to you or, for the person fishing, the feeling of being at one with the river and the river voices.

The Holy Man

When my father had been given notice that time was running out on him, the local 'holy man', as he was affectionately known, came to visit; came to pray and to weep, to make connections with the other side, to let them know of my father's pressing need.

Later that afternoon when I called in, my father confided that he had availed of the 'ministrations' of the holy man. Without much thought but with encouragement in mind, I countered with, 'but sure you're a holy man yourself'.

He was having none of it. Quick as you like, his words stood up to me. 'I'm a hypocrite,' he said, matter-of-factly, neither put-down nor self-diminishment intended, as though he were talking about the weather, quite unaware of how his admission justified him in the eyes of God as did the tax-collector's humble prayer from the back of the temple (Luke 18:9).

It was one of those rare moments. Any awkwardness or in-admission between us vanished. I was properly small again in his presence. And he didn't want a response. He was happy just to say what he may have wanted to hear himself say for a long time, less a confession than a liberating awareness to be confirmed in. Then, on a roll, he added, 'I was a dreamer all my life,' and with a smile, 'but a dreamer lives forever; a toiler dies in a day.'

Laughter at l'Arche

[W]ithout a word, the Hindu hermit lifted his arms as if he would touch the sky and with a wide downward sweep assured Abhishiktananda (a fellow monk) that God was wonderfully good and all he could desire, and both men laughed together a glorious heaven-filled laugh.
Murray Rogers

It cannot be true that Jesus never laughed, yet he's seldom portrayed laughing. Artistic impressions favour a serious look, the disappointment on his face. I know of only one picture – sent by Tessie from the Philippines – where he's shown laughing his head off. Far from being irreverent, it shows a man really enjoying his life. 'Consider the lilies,' he was fond of saying; they just open up and express themselves.

If we could trust life a little more instead of trying to control every aspect of it, we might allow our guiding Angel a bit of elbow room and learn that everything does not depend on us. Spiritual people laugh a lot because they know that everything is in God's hands – they don't need to be afraid.

Jean Vanier records that the early days of l'Arche (communities of care which he founded for the most vulnerable people), were times of 'immense laughter'. Not laughter as ridicule and telling jokes but the laughter of human beings at what foolish children we are, how little we understand, but how much we are loved. The kind of laughter that celebrates difference, makes communion, breaks the bread.

Chinese Friends

The trees are wearing less and less. It's the autumn collection. A small girl in a red jumper and grey skirt detaches from her mother to go back and pick up a giant, colourful, maple leaf for school.

My Chinese friend, Long Weng, phones to say we must meet up but I am too tired. My energy is down to a trickle. I decide rather to visit Dr Wang, the acupuncturist, and Teresa, his assistant, who translates for him.

We talk a little and then I lie down as he applies ten or twelve needles along the sluggish pathways, following an invisible map that, on his wall chart, looks like the Milky Way arranged in a human shape. They leave me then, as parents would, and turn out the light. I drift off to sleep with a thread of Oriental music in the background.

An hour later, I close the door with three bags of herbs and a feeling of well-being, of having been cared for. As I leave, I know that another person is beginning to tell her particular trouble and that Dr Wang will smile and talk directly to her in Chinese as if she could understand him. I always like that touch.

Down on the street, human and mechanical traffic is flowing. I feel young again and notice the colour at my feet. I remember the High Infant this morning in her red and grey bending low in wonder at a leaf. Then I return the call to Long and arrange a time.

Those Who Carry Pianos

There's a meditation in Buddhism called *tonglen*. It's a way to practice compassion. On the in-breath, you breathe a particular suffering into your heart, imagining it, perhaps, as a black and gooey substance. Then you breathe your peace and goodness out in the form of light and healing energy to the one in pain. Your body prays, your heart becomes a sacred heart.

When faced with some awful situation, it is tempting to move away (and not inhale), and often we may need to do just that. An alternative, however, might be to take a deliberate breath and invite the Spirit (whose Hebrew name means *Breath*) to breathe through us, so that, in the words of Anna Kamienska, 'Those who carry pianos to the tenth floor, wardrobes and coffins, will all be lifted like a gull's feather, like a dry leaf.'

Whether we know it or not, we breathe in, pause, breathe out, over and over, with every creature (from bacteria to whale), and with trees and plants, too, which deserve our gratitude for supplying us with the oxygen we need to live. For all of us together share in that loving Breath of Life, a breath we can trust to fill the sail of our small craft and blow us beyond our limited horizons.

From such communion, compassion grows; from compassion, communion.

Three-Legged Race

My weak knee is telling me something; go slow, take careful steps, no sudden turns! As the Buddhist might say, 'Lay your foot gently on the earth.' A hard call when from boyhood I have preferred to run rather than walk.

Now I must learn to walk. Learn to esteem my knees and other joints. And indeed give thanks to the inner workings of my body – to my heart, faithful companion, beating its way through my life, to my lungs, to my gut which knows so well how to discriminate.

All of us hobble through, despite our delusions of poise and swagger; some, it would appear, with a splinter of the Cross catching their breath at every step. It seems that we have to carry each other or maybe just agree to move awkwardly together over rough ground as though we are tied in a three-legged race!

But this race is not run or won in normal time. It takes place in longings and endurance, in stand-offs and detours far from a finishing line. Deep in that struggle we believe that there is shelter in love's welcoming embrace.

May the Spirit lighten your journey with encouragement, the Son clear a path for you and may the Father open wide his arms to break your fall.

Beloved

This evening, three babies have come to be baptised. They have brought their families with them; three bright stars showing the way; three angels singing 'peace on earth' to the gobsmacked company.

Emmeline, Bronson, Jetta Lily. Welcome. A word, a wish, a cry. A little oil for beginners signed on the chest to say that Christ is your brother now and will fight your corner. And for the shepherds, these questions: Will you show these children how to love? Will you teach them to pray? *Emmeline, Bronson, Jetta Lily*, I baptise you in the name of Loving Communion.

The white crocheted shawl is opened out in welcome. The oil of chrism, blessed and sweetened with herbs last Holy Thursday, is spread in a cross on a carefree forehead, saying, 'You are the beloved of God.' A father reaches out and takes a light from the Easter candle standing to attention.

Does christening matter? Does it add anything? Only the heart knows how it works its magic as we leave on light feet, our heads in the air. And what if no one remembers much about it? My aunt Mary, who held my newborn head over the font, says that I slept through it all, which is considered a point in my favour! That's the beauty of it. It's all really play as we recall Jesus and his cousin John splashing in the river Jordan and over them a voice calling, 'Child!'

Whistleblower

I dropped into a city centre church one morning and was amazed to see a man balancing, in his bare feet, on top of a pew in front of Our Lady! What kept a small group of onlookers speechless was the fact that, in attempting to reach out to her from that position, he had to lean across a tier of lit candles that flickered close to his feet!

He was deep in concentration as I approached and suggested that he climb down as he could burn himself. He glared at me the way a prophet would. 'Stop it,' he said, 'you're interrupting me. I have work to do.' I acknowledged my intrusion, backed off and left him to it. I didn't want to be around to see him removed by people in uniform.

His bare feet and his comment about 'having work to do' stayed with me. Afterwards, when I wrote this poem I had this troubled man in mind, whistle-blowing on all our safe ways and what passes for religious sanity!

> He had long hair that was greying,
> held a paper sword that he waved
> at passers-by who didn't laugh
> when his weapon blunted and the daft
> look heightened in his eyes. In his cap
> the coins amounted to little; small drops
> of rain quietened him. Inside the church
> a bank of candles glowed and smoked.
> He could temper his blade there, compose
> himself, lunge, startle his own shadow.

Soul Singing

Only last week I was walking in the city with a friend when I overheard her singing to herself. I said nothing at the time for any comment would have been an intrusion and would certainly have ended the melody. Later, I realised that for those precious moments she had been audibly in tune with herself; body, mind and spirit singing as one.

In Papua New Guinea, the local languages describe soul as 'the seed of singing'. In those terms, singing then must be the soul in flower! Some cultures believe that the evolving universe is sung into being. So imagine that. The Creator Spirit singing her way in and out of harmonies beyond us and beauty breaking out in the most amazing forms of life.

I don't want to live in a world where remote controls rule and new gadgets promise to make something of me. I want to live with my ears unplugged so that they can hear the music of the earth, with my eyes ranging beyond the bewitching screen, my hands free to take someone's hand instead of incessantly texting.

We can guess why St Francis sang with the birds and why the birds sang with him. He was simply in tune with who he was in God's eyes, a creature born to overhear the song of fellow creatures and recognise it as his own, as variations on a theme of presence and thanks.

Deaf Musician

It's an image I recall from time to time, that of the deaf musician who goes on playing to please his master although there is little enjoyment in it for himself. It comes from Francis de Sales writing about how a person might respond to the mystery of love. It's clearly not about 'job satisfaction' or the line, 'what's in it for me?'

This kind of understanding may be old-fashioned now like the prayer that intercedes for someone to be made well though the loved one dies. Or begs that world suffering be lessened, a hope that shatters next morning in the heartbreak of headlines.

Maybe it's better to think of it in terms of play. A child plays for no other reason than to play. There is no additional outcome foreseen, 'We're just playing, Mum.'

Sometimes I notice people in a church stopping at the statues of various saints. They may light a candle or just touch a cold hand or hem affectionately. They are playing the part of the deaf musician. They believe that someone is listening though they can't hear their own music; they trust that all will be well though they don't know how the story ends.

A prayer is a bit of good news about life, a confidence 'that everything will be clear', a gesture towards the heart that beats within creation – that sacred heart whose heartbeat you can't quite distinguish from your own.

The Fox and Prince

*Unless you have wasted time in a city, you cannot
pretend to know it well*
Julian Green

Nor is the slow lane about laziness but about the
carefree movement of someone prepared to dawdle,
amble, ensure that time should not have the last word.
To have acquired a sense of belonging implies that you
have at some time idled on a corner, in a café, or on a
park bench. 'When it's over', writes Mary Oliver, 'I don't
want to end up simply having visited the world.'

Someone who has leaned against a city wall while
waiting on a bus has left an impression of closeness
there that says we belong together, even need each
other, that we know something (however unsayable) of
the other.

A particular morning will come back to you later in life
(when you 'don't go out much any more'), of a Saturday,
perhaps, when you would add distance and unfamiliar
streets to your route in pursuit of a particular flavour of
coffee and a comforting ambience. Or a memory will
revive of church bells above light traffic, lopping off the
quarter hours for anyone with an ear for discarded time
as it swells into something else in your heart. And you
will say 'thanks'.

Antoine de Saint-Exupéry leaves it to the fox to explain
this secret to the Little Prince: 'It is the time you have
wasted on your rose that makes your rose so important
… You become responsible forever for what you have
tamed.'

Street Mime Artist

for Joe Lucey

A man dressed all in gold is standing on a city street. He
doesn't move. He is a statue and can stand still while
about him traffic flows and people swerve to avoid each
other. Then somebody stops and drops a coin in his cup
and is rewarded with a sweet!

I spotted him one day making his way through town, on
his way to work – top hat, gold coat, painted gold face,
dragging a case behind him. How can he stand for so
long, I wonder, without blinking? Is he blank inside?
Does he sometimes want to give up and stretch his legs,
scatter the pretence, throw up the job?

The poet, John Milton, in his blindness discovered, after
much complaint to the Almighty, that 'they also serve
who only stand and wait'. He could have written that for
our man.

Perhaps the street artist, sharpening his ability to be still,
enjoys the satisfaction of surprising a distracted
passerby with a conspiratorial wink or the lift of an
eyebrow. He (or she) is playing a game with us, inviting
us to stop for a moment on a busy high street and smile;
and maybe recall a child tottering in her mother's heels
imagining what it's like to be grown up.

Then I remember how I found my car keys eventually
(after a morning's search) by just standing still. Could
that be what he is miming for us, 'rejoice with me; I have
found what was lost'?

Wake-Up Call

Too often we see the spot on the wall but miss the wall. We see a blemish but miss the beauty of a face. We get addicted to the fault, become obsessive about what's wrong with the world. One of the accusations that Jesus made of the serious-minded, the fault-finders, was that they wouldn't join in! It's hard to be critical of the dancers when we ourselves are dancing. Nor can we enjoy the water by standing on the side of the pool, making excuses and blaming others for splashing.

It's possible to spend our whole life asleep (by the side of the pool or on the edge of the dance floor). It's true that we wake up each morning but often the eyes of our heart never see the light of day. A plank of fear, of mistrust, of inherited bias, of unquestioned belief, of living only for the approval of others can board up the windows. And the joy of *being alive* escapes us.

At our core, however, is a child of grace, a gift of the universe who, according to psalm 139, is 'beautifully and wonderfully made'. Wow!

Jesus warned the religious people of his time not to get caught up in the details. Sabbaths, he said, are not pigeon-holes on a calendar but times to learn compassion for ourselves and for every other fellow pilgrim – tree, spider, frog, snake.

An Eyewash for the Eye

Looking at a drawing by the American abstract artist Agnes Martin is, at first, like looking at the intersecting lines on a sheet of graph paper. It would be easy to pass it by and say, 'Where's the art in that?' Her intention, however, isn't to draw something so much as to open up a space – like a desert in New Mexico, say (where she lived on her own) – before which you might pause long enough to *see into*.

A simple, direct gaze is necessary to lead us in, she says, like crossing 'an empty beach to look at the ocean'. Visiting an art gallery could be described as an eyewash for the eye which enables you to see afresh, to move slowly like someone lost in contemplation. You exit with the gift of new sight.

For the first men to land on the moon in 1969, their new perspective allowed them to see the Earth from the outside. And what a revelation that was! It brought tears to their eyes to witness something never seen before – our fragile home place floating like a blue ball in the immensity of space.

'Nature is like parting a curtain; you go into it. I want to draw a certain response like this,' Agnes has written, 'not a specific response but that quality of response from people when they leave themselves behind, often experienced in nature – an experience of simple joy.'

Winter

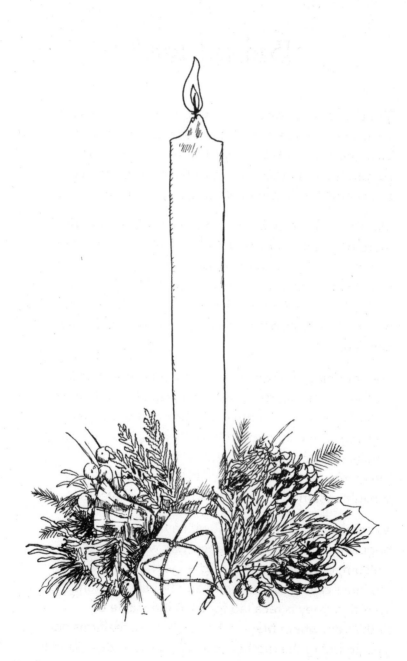

Baby Light

To our ancestors who built Newgrange five thousand years ago, the realities of day and night were profound. With the cold and darkness deepening and food in short supply, the winter solstice must have been greeted with a welcome the depth of which we can barely imagine.

Our times are so different though our questions are more or less the same. Of course, we, who have almost lost the art of looking up, couldn't hold a candle to their knowledge of the night skies nor match their wonder-stirred hearts before the renewal of the sun's covenant with earth and its promise of springtime and harvest and new life.

The returning sun was their sustaining hope, their reason, on the shortest day of the year, to direct the first rays of morning through a light-box and down along a pathway to the inner chamber. We can guess at fertility parallels – the piercing light, the receptive womb and the community's place within that cosmic liturgy as sunlight resumed its power and darkness deferred.

To combine December light with a newborn baby is beguiling. Our Stone Age ancestors would have welcomed baby light in Newgrange, having prepared the inner cave as a sheltering and holding gesture. That sacred journey is recalled for us in the stable of Bethlehem where Mary, in her birth cries, reaffirms her 'yes' to being the mother of Jesus, the one described by John as 'the light' in whom creation rejoices.

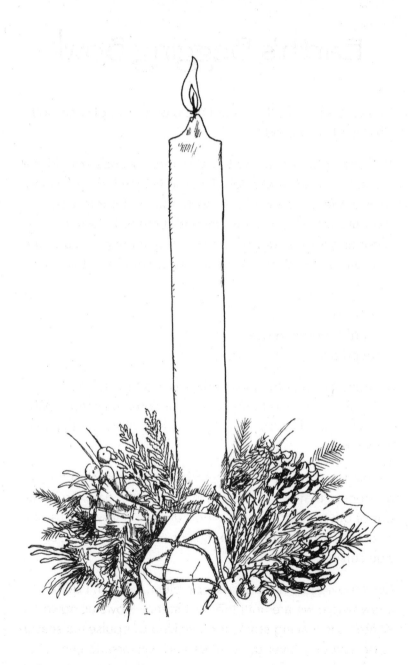

Earth's Begging Bowl

The cartoon read, 'I've spent most of my life playing golf. The rest I've wasted!'

I'm looking at the leaves building into mounds around the trees. It started weeks ago. Now, in November, it's raining leaves. We are blessed with such notice of our (super) natural world. Trees know when it's time to hibernate. The mounting leaves suggest a time for quietness and a chance to breathe. Another season advances with its gift and threat.

> leaf fall –
> earth's begging bowl
> overflows

'Fortune Favours the Fast', advertises a broadband company. We need to speed up our communication. We need to speed up our lives. We have so much to do and so little time!

Yet we have everything we need to be alive except the awareness that we *are* alive. On a particular date we came out of our mother's womb. Another date will sweep us out of time. Christ's coming reminds us that the light of our true selves shines in us.

On a moving train the landscape blurs. We don't quite know where we are until the next station slows us down. Winter is for taking stock, for checking our pulse – a season to be savoured over cups of tea and conversation; in warmer clothes; in longer silences with the whole of bowed-down creation before the One who is our light.

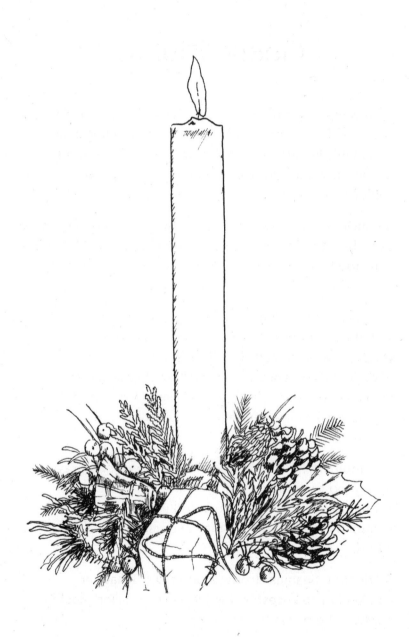

Geese Flying

I just saw something wonderful. Geese flying in that V-shape high over me. I looked out through falling snow and marvelled at their sense of purpose. They were a family – birds of a feather – and they were going somewhere.

Meanwhile I sit in, watching snow building snow-shapes over the city and asking myself, 'Should I go out?' 'Need I change from shoes to boots?' Wondering when will the cold spell end.

The geese honking their way through the air delight with their livingness, their otherness, their nearness to us. Even when human speech fails, our heart can be lifted in the presence of these fellow-creatures with whom we share this living space. *Have they suddenly registered a snow-thought and decided to move elsewhere?*

This moment moves me into a part of myself that says, 'It is good to be here,' and away from the part that continually worries. I am reminded that I can no more control the days of my life than understand the flight of a bird.

A line from Seamus Heaney's poem 'At Banagher' concerning an ancestor, 'the journeyman tailor', could apply to the geese this morning:

'The way is opener for your being in it.'

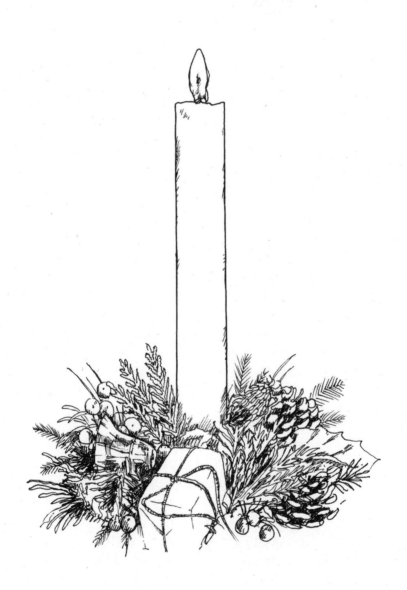

Four Days

I wonder what it would have been like not to have been the eldest boy. I mean if my brother had lived. His was a rough birth, I'm told, having to be hauled out eventually by the leg. Needless to say, the battering did him no good and, four days later, 'having refused to play ball with the authorities', he was sent to the back of the class in the Angels' Plot in Glasnevin.

He couldn't cry, my mother said, though my parents made up for that with their endless tears. I think of him mischievously, being interrogated by the medical staff but refusing to comply; a baby dissident, an infant behind the lines.

Maybe four days is enough to get your point across, to deliver the message, to make the connection. Still I wonder what it would have been like to have had him to look up to. Maybe I could have dodged some of the assumed responsibility that attends the firstborn girl and boy.

In her poem 'Annunciation' Anna Kamienska has a line which says, 'Nobody can know what loneliness looks like when the angel is gone.' She is talking about Mary's strange meeting with the angel Gabriel who tells her that she will give birth to a baby named Jesus who is the Messiah. Then he leaves her. In that moment she is every woman who has ever known the piercing loneliness of having held an angel in her arms and then lost him.

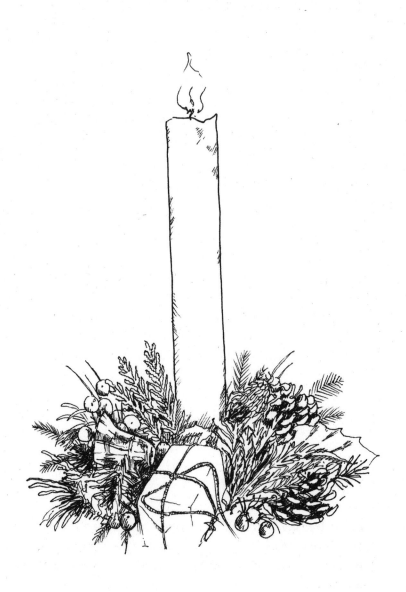

It is Finished in Beauty

There is a tender moment in Bernard O'Donoghue's poem 'In Millstreet Hospital' where he recounts visiting his cousin, 'who doesn't wake up much, nor … seem to see the green mountain framed in the window'. On his way out, a man is sitting by the door – 'stick, well-knotted tie, watch-chain, tweed jacket' – with a question for him: 'Excuse my troubling you, but would you be going anywhere near a railway station?' A smiling nurse steps in: 'Maybe tomorrow, James, maybe tomorrow …'

The Navajo Indians pray 'in beauty may I walk' as their commitment to living in harmony with all that is and of being at home on the earth. The prayer concludes, 'In old age, wandering on a trail of beauty, lively, may I walk. In old age, wandering on a trail of beauty, living again, may I walk. It is finished in beauty. It is finished in beauty.'

I find a recent diary entry:
Called home. Met my mother at the door. She was dressed in a matching blouse and cardigan of cerise. She had just had her hair done and looked all set for the road. When I left her at 5.15, the man on the telly had dealt at £6,000 and seemed relieved. We stood and looked at the sky from the doorway. There was a lovely sunset. 'That's how you know the west,' I said, for something to say. I drove off but it stayed with me – the flame she was wearing and the clouds on fire!

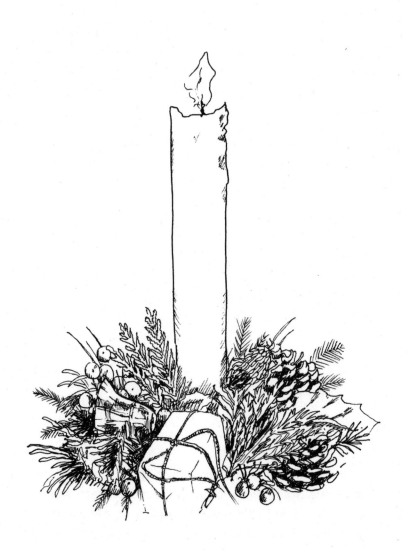

Bud

I am sitting on a train waiting for the journey to begin. Travelling this way has to be one of life's luxuries. You settle yourself in, then, like a seasoned traveller, place on the table your phone, glasses, bottle of water and a book.

Today it's crowded, though not enough to disturb the upbeat anticipation of the journey; countryside, tea from the trolley service, time to read.

A young man enters with four cans of Bud in a plastic bag and sits beside me. He has had a few already and is eager to talk – sport, work, places we might have in common. I ask about his family. His mother, late forties, is wheelchair-bound. He feels deeply for her, says she can't talk now, only smile. It grieves him. He snaps another can.

Cans finished, we're nearing the end of the line. He's going on to meet a friend for a last drink. We smile, shake hands again, for the fourth time, 'You'll say one for her.' 'Of course I will.' Then he's off down the platform.

Nothing dramatic. Just life and how it goes. Somewhere between one point and another we make contact, share a few words, a joke, all the while suspecting the weight of living each one carries as we break the bread of our common humanity together.

What Love Does

Each November we recall the story of a young Martin of Tours who sliced through his cloak to share one half with a naked beggar. And how that night in a dream Jesus appeared to him wearing the piece of garment he had given away!

On a cold windy day in March we might also think of Francis stripping off before his wealthy father and the bishop of Assisi to announce publicly that from then on he belonged to the company of the poor Christ and would rely on the heavenly Father's care!

Centuries on, Martin and Francis still light our path. Though their gestures are extravagant, they point to the small deed done with great love. Like the poor widow in the Temple whom Jesus noticed dropping two copper coins into the treasury. 'She has put in more than anyone,' he says, because, unlike the others who contribute out of their abundance, she puts in 'her whole living'.

It is the small, thoughtful action that can change a life or at least a day in a life. In the words of Patrick Kavanagh, 'There is nothing as dead and damned as an important thing. The things that really matter are casual, insignificant, little things, things you would be ashamed to talk of publicly.'

Like making room for someone in a conversation or sharing a croissant!

In the Father's House

Today I am meeting with friends of Michael who attend 'the Father's House' in Skipton (a coffee shop by day), where every Thursday evening they gather up the fragments of their lives. In the words of the beloved disciple they admit 'it is the Lord' who is their sustenance and blessing. It's about love, they say, about allowing oneself to be touched by love. I notice the absence of ego and competition in them. These are friends; they sing a hymn to friendship by the way they greet, meet and share.

They remind me of what it is all about; what remains, in other words, when you take the religious scaffolding away. They pray in a coffee shop, break the bread of real communion and practice the art of forgiveness. As a consequence they discover a deep freedom and move out spontaneously to people in need.

They become fathers again – maybe real fathers for the first time – nurturing, affirming and confirming the good in everyone. Christianity has become for them a way of fathering, breathing the Spirit over each one, receiving the Spirit from each other. They use ordinary means – a text, a hug, a deep listening in, a word that builds up, a hand that forgives, a look that says 'you are in the Father's heart and all is well'.

Go there sometime soon. The Father's House is everywhere!

Darling God

At eighteen years, on a mid-winter day of snow,
Nicholas Herman stood before a gaunt and leafless tree
and imagined how in the spring it would almost liquefy
into leaf. It was an experience that moved him (literally)
to take off his shoes; in 1666 he joined the barefooted
Carmelites at Paris! As community cook, (newly-named)
Brother Lawrence discovered that God could be as
present to him in his noisy kitchen as in the chapel – as
before a leafless tree …

Dear God, why do we dress you up in the worst of
ourselves: 'all-powerful, lord of hosts'; your imminent
return a scold to frighten us; 'just wait 'til your father
gets home!'

Darling God, we want to turn your love into language
and law, confine your presence within the boundaries of
human speech.

But what does the crow say? Can we hear you in his
caw? Are you slow like the tree in bud? Is your voice
silky like leaves or succulent like water?

The wisest of us know the limitations of language and
choose the pillow talk of the long night to speak your
name, 'sweetheart', 'angel', 'love', or a sigh, 'God is very
good to me.'

This morning I listen to you falling as rain and breaking
over Liberty House in the cry and laughter of gulls, in
the bleat of a train from Connolly, in the sound of
someone in the kitchen.

Angels at St James'

'They couldn't be paid enough,' my brother-in-law confides and I wholeheartedly agree. Standing in the Acute A & E, it seems that a nurse is expected to be both busy and still at the same time, to be a sage, a seer, able to call up the precise healing word, to use a hoist, be calm in a storm.

The Good Samaritan comes to mind: how he stops and looks, then acts – salves and bandages the bloodied man, lifts him up and arranges his convalescence.

This man is the neighbour, par excellence. Even his enemy is not beyond the reach of his compassion. Nor any other creature, one might suggest, endangered by prejudice and disrespect!

Still the war goes on. We make new enemies and keep the old, 'mind our own business' as we classify, reclassify, generalise – 'they're all the same.' The Samaritan stops and sees the broken body of a man and recognises it as his own. 'Though there are torturers in the world,' writes Michael Coady, 'there are also musicians.' And, he might have added, nurses!

An elderly patient takes my arm, 'I was at death's door last time' and for a moment I imagine him standing outside with a doctor's note in his hand, then deciding not to knock!

In the gathering dusk, they are arriving for the night vigil; they will keep watch during the small hours, when resolve is low, and speak someone's name to reassure him.

Made in the East

Some years ago, I came across my father's straw hat and took it with me on holidays. From a certain angle, I could see that it still held something of him. He had fancied himself in that.

For some reason, I recalled reading of how St Francis de Sales once went to visit the Shroud of Turin on a hot day and how a drop of sweat from his brow had fallen onto it. The attendant was clearly annoyed at the carelessness shown by the bishop. Commenting on this incident later, Francis remarked that a sick child was often wrapped in his father's coat in the belief that a father's love could be passed on in this way. Surely then, he mused, the Shroud which had covered the dead body of Jesus would gladly absorb the sweat of a disciple.

Maybe a similar instinct caused my father of a winter's night to throw his heavy coat on my bed to add some extra warmth and the reassurance of a father's care. The same instinct that moved a sick woman to touch 'even the hem' of Jesus' clothes believing she would be healed. And she was because she had truly touched *him*.

Clothes have their stories, too. How this T-shirt, for instance, journeyed from the East where it was made, how small the fingers were, how hot it was in the factory and how drops of sweat fell …

Brógeen

The invitation, *can't you stay awhile?* comes from a deep place. To ask it is to reveal your need of someone's presence. It is to show your hand – like Jesus did after his resurrection: his battered hand.

Most of us believe we haven't time to stay, to sit, to listen. There are things to do – programmes, meetings, deadlines. And maybe when someone asks us to stay we are suddenly aware of how busy we are and move along.

'Stay' we say to the dog and suspect by his response that he is living more mindfully than we are! In the following, I try to imagine it from Brógeen's side:

> *This bundle of dog racing up and down the beach*
> *wants so badly to sleep within hearing of a human*
> *voice.*
> *His great sadness – how deep our failure to simply be*
> *there at the window sometimes, to open up, play. Stay.*

'Tomorrow' we'll make time to play, to laugh, to read that book, to write, to visit. Then, one day, tomorrow comes and we suddenly notice how years have passed; that we have walked out as far as the turn. We are now on the journey home.

No one can take away our unique pain but someone who stays can reassure us that we are not alone as Love sits down with us and extends a hand.

An Post

Days before Christmas I find myself part of a long queue in the post office snaking its way along as one by one we are called forward, 'Counter number 4 please.' We share a common purpose; we want to make contact with those far away, to sign our name to a card and write 'love and best wishes'.

And then it's over to *An Post* to do its magic, to spirit our mail to towns and villages across the planet. In a day or two a card will drop through a letterbox and someone will check for a familiar hand. The wonder of it all – *par avion* – never leaves me.

To my right, a girl is sealing up a box with sellotape in the way a spider wraps a fly, turning it over and over. 'Must be something precious,' I say, but she doesn't hear.

The story of Pat Molloy, the postman, whose son is living somewhere in America comes back to me. The family has lost touch with him. No letter comes, though Christmas after Christmas his father goes on his rounds with an eye out for a US stamp. Here is heartbreak in motion – the tramp of footsteps up the path to a neighbour's house and a barking dog.

In the cave of the heart a light flickers. It must not go out. Even the stars look tearful on a frosty night. 'Look up. Hold on!'

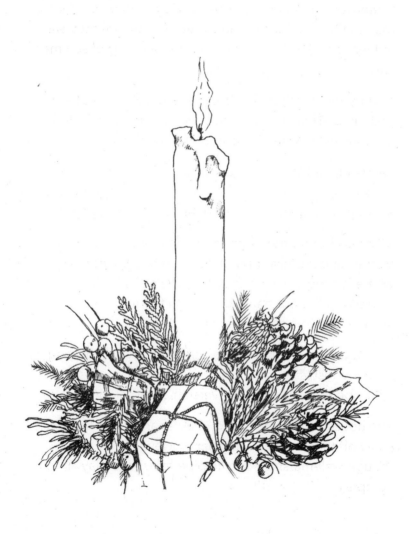

Kinlough Stream

It seems only yesterday since we walked that country road in the company of the whispering stream that was hidden, covered in as it was with the layering of summer leaves.

And remember then at a break in the trees it was louder and rambled on in a language we didn't have words for though we knew its consolation from way back.

We would fall silent then and listen and almost hear ourselves listening. (That is a fine moment, to know you are enjoying the moment even as you are enjoying it.)

That was before they started building and clearing ditches and corralling the stream into a cement gully where it struggles now to convey its melody with something like the heartache which the Israelites felt when asked to sing their songs in exile.

Boxed-in, the interplay of soil and root and shadowing leaves is lost. The water is heard now as a tuneless tune, a blubbering, a poor cover version of the original.

The houses are up, the road is wider and busy. Low walls show off the estates. To my ear, however, the water though well-marshalled in its pipe refuses to play. It complains.

Tree Talk

All the trees of the wood shout for joy
Psalm 95

That buzzing you hear is a chainsaw removing trees from the end of what used to be convent property. The city council has other plans for it now as a building site – somewhere with no need of trees. Saturday is the chosen day and a man arrives to take them down, measuring them into blocks for firing. It will take a couple of hours, at most, to clear the place and load up his truck.

Meanwhile, it being January, nobody is about, a face only drawn away momentarily from the TV by the nuisance of a whining blade. It is a mark of sensitivity to respect trees, to recognise their mystery and rootedness, their presence as a word of God. It is said that the sound most dreaded by Colmcille in Iona was of an axe chopping in his beloved Derry wood.

Today these things don't seem to matter. Tree flesh is hard and doesn't feel a thing; it has no appetite for life, we say, no sense of smell, of sight, hearing, of what it means to be alive. Science today, however, is telling us otherwise; trees know well what is going on!

It doesn't take long with a chainsaw. In no time the truck is ready to head off with our trees that only this morning tossed in the wind and drank in rain. The young man takes out his smartphone to make a call, 'Job's done, see you then.'

Water Tables

I pour some water in the sink as I need to shave, then step back and imagine it for what it could be – a holy well – this layer of water which I hardly notice in my headlong rush towards what comes next.

By the time I return to the sink the water is cold. To my awakened imagination it now appears as a water font. So I dip my fingers in and bless myself in the name of all that is parched, knowing that in a refugee camp a fight is breaking out over access to the one pump supplying a hundred families. As a tiny gesture I take some water to the plants. My prayer plant, in the act of unfolding new leaves these days, is glad of a drop.

If we could only get in touch with the stillness each plant inhabits we might recover our own stillness. There is a life-giving well inside us. Christians call it Christ and recall a well in Samaria where Jesus talked with a woman about her need to find 'living water' so she would never be thirsty again. Holy wells echo that promise.

I square up to the mirror, release the cold and refill the sink from the hot tap. In my youth I wriggled down a pothole in Dunmore caves and entered a huge cavern sloping to a pool of still water. We swished our torches and didn't stay long; emerged a little breathless (and relieved) into the light.

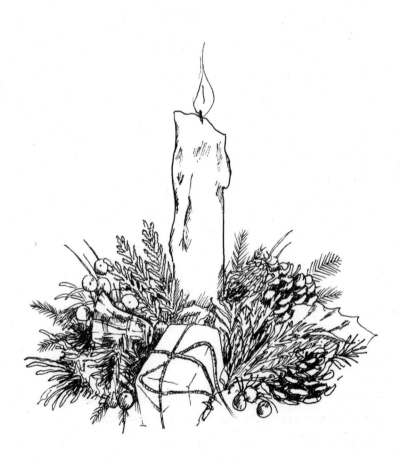

Two Clocks

A friend has been telling me of a conversation she witnessed between two older women as they talked the small talk of life – what was happening beyond the doorstep, who was looking bad or who had mended up well – their words like frothy bubbles dancing over the dark.

It took her back years, she said, to hear the clock ticking behind them and having its own say, which reminded me of Seamus Heaney's poem recalling his Aunt Mary in her white floury apron and 'the scone rising to the tick of two clocks'.

That memory evokes from him the tender sigh, 'here is a space', and makes me think of Eucharist where words fall away and there is love unspoken.

In the interval it takes the scone to rise, the clock ticks. 'Your life is over like a sigh,' chimes the writer of the psalm.

The women talk, their short sentences trailing over the silence and the pain of life as they take a little drink to lift the heart.

That's all. Just a space for being together, for having the time of their lives, for dropping crumbs without a second thought.

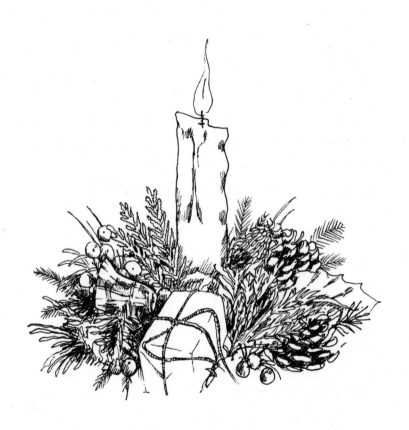

Scraps for the Feast

'This little bit won't matter'
Edward Echlin

Our generation has grown up with no appetite for leftovers. One third of all our food is thrown out. The plate is not cleared, crooked vegetables are discarded along with the cheese considered too close to the 'best by' date. You would think that a country which has experienced famine would have a heightened respect for the fruits of the earth – but we forget.

First thing this morning, I notice the robin still feeding where we broke some bread for him yesterday. He has an eye for the tiniest crumb. 'Gather up the scraps', the Master said, 'so that nothing will be lost.' And they filled twelve baskets with the crusts.

Recently, I read of a community of people who at the end of the day place any extra bread in a bag and hang it outside their door for another hungry person to share. It's a sign of unawareness that we can sit down to eat and not acknowledge these gifts as Grace. It would profoundly change our attitude to the source of our food if we could take a moment or two to recognise what's there – chicken or chickpea, salmon or salad and to imagine the bounce of lamb in a field or root vegetables lifted up in thanksgiving with the crumbs of clay still clinging to them.

'The practice of the Eucharist is a practice of awareness,' writes the Buddhist monk, Thich Nhat Hanh. We only know what bread is when we have lingered over it.

All the Time in the World

New Year's Day – sunlight and honey in a jar

We sat together, Jane, Ronan and I, around a small table with three medium cappuccinos which we clinked as it was New Year's Day and freezing outside. We hadn't met in a while but it didn't matter. There was no distance between us and soon we were talking our way back into ourselves, listening to one another, waiting for the right word to fall into place.

This seems to be what Rublev's famous icon of the Trinity, with three young men sitting at a table, is hinting at. That God is good conversation and to be in God is to be present to each other (of any species) in a completely affirming way. Our bodies crave such conversation but often we have to make do with designer chat and sound bite. We seldom get to chew on the bones of who we are.

'How are you?' we say in greeting. But when that question is really meant as 'how are you deep down?' it is very different. It says 'I have time to listen if you want to tell me; all the time in the world.' A friend will ask it like that. Of course you can't put the answer into words alone but you have a sense that your life is held as sacred for that moment and that you are loved. When God sits down with us at table the conversation is good, time lets us be … lets us be.

Snowdrops

'I just saunter down the road now,' mother says, as though she has settled on a new way of going; her outer journey seeming to mirror some inner one. It's a lovely word, its sound suggesting that easy, loose-shouldered, measured pace which allows time to stand with a neighbour and smile.

The word is French; the origin less certain. Were the Sainte Terre pilgrims on their way to the Holy Land or were they drifters, 'sans terre', without a place of their own?

Although Jesus was heading towards Jerusalem, he often appears to be sauntering around with a band of followers, stopping to teach, to listen and to heal. I think of Basho, too, poet and wandering monk, writing himself into literary history on his 'travel sketches', his haiku all light and weightlessness.

Or Robert Walser whose lines I love, attempting (without success) to walk his way out of darkness: 'I have seen snowdrops in gardens and on the cart of a peasant woman who was driving to market. I wanted to buy a bouquet from her, but thought it not right for a robust man like me to ask for so tender a thing.'

Is it all sauntering? And does it matter to people on the road, aware of what lies ahead but investing it with the significance of a laugh, a sigh, a line.

I was going to pick flowers; now I leave them all standing and walk home an old man.
Hermann Hesse

One For the Road

Don't you remember how after the evening reception
two young friends slipped him out the side door
for one last drink, his polished box making its way
daintily as the small wheels of the coffin trolley twisted
down the path. 'A last mouthful of city air', they said,
'and a pint of stout', to be poured by the barman
over his name plate while the locals clapped and cheered.
To be fair, Fr Casey made light of it on their return
and drew out deeper meanings next morning about being
neighbours and rites of passage, recognising the episode
as no more than a small irreverence – stealing a mate
back to themselves when it seemed that Jennings had
him.

Bibliography

Paul Auster, *True Tales of American Life*, Faber and Faber Ltd, 2002.

Liberty Hyde Bailey, *The Holy Earth: Towards a New Environmental Ethic*, Dover Publications, NY, 2009 (first published in 1915).

Bishop, Elizabeth, 'Manners', *Complete Poems*, Chatto & Windus, 2004.

Rachel Carson, *Silent Spring*, Penguin Books, 1965.

Carlson, Richard, *Don't Sweat the Small Stuff ... and it's all Small Stuff*, Hodder Mobius, 1998.

Coady, Michael, 'Though There Are Torturers' in *Essential Poems From The Staying Alive Trilogy*, Neil Astley, ed., Bloodaxe Books, 2012.

Dalai Lama quoting from essay, 'The Paradox of Our Age' in *Words Aptly Spoken; Collection of Prayers, Homilies and Monologues*, Dr Moorehead, 1995.

de Saint-Exupery, Antoine, *The Little Prince*, Reynal and Hitchcock, 1943.

Echlin, Edward P., *Live Simply: Let Others Live*, Progressio, London, 2007.

Feehan, John, *The Singing Heart of the World*, The Columba Press, 2010.

Green, Julian, *Paris*, Penguin Books, 1991.

Greenlaw, Lavinia, 'Essex Rag' from collection *Minsk*, Faber and Faber, 2003.

Hahn, Thich Nhat, *Peace is Every Step: the Practice of Mindfulness in Everyday Life*, Rider, Random House, 1995.

Hardie, Kerry, 'She Replies to Carmel's Letter' in *Cry for the Hot Belly*, Gallery Press, Co. Meath, 2000.

Heaney Seamus, 'Mossbawn: Two Poems in Dedication: 1 Sunlight', 'Fosterling', 'The Swing', 'At Banagher' in *Opened Ground: Poems 1966-1996*, Faber and Faber, 1998.

Hesse, Hermann, 'The First Flowers' in *Poems*, Jonathan Cape, 1977.

Higashida, Naoki, *The Reason I Jump*, Random House, 2013.

Hopkins, Gerard Manley, 'God's Grandeur', *Poems and Prose of Gerard Manley Hopkins*, Penguin Books, 1953.

Jeffers, Robinson, 'Carmel Point', *The Selected Poetry of Robinson Jeffers*, Stanford University Press, 1988.

Kamieńska, Anna, 'Annunciation' and 'Those Who Carry' from *Two Darknesses*, Flambard, 1994.

Laing, R.D., *The Critical Psychology of R.D. Laing* by Carl Ratner, Telos, Vol. 5, 1970.

Martin, Agnes, quotations from *'3 X Abstractions: New Methods of Drawing, Hilma Af Klint, Emma Kunz, Agnes Martin*, eds Cathering de Zegher, Hendel Teicher, The Drawing Centre, NY, 2005.

Masefield, John, 'Tewkesbury Road' in *Poems of To-Day: an Anthology*, Sidgwick & Jackson, 1915.

Meegan, Michael, *All Will Be Well*, Eye Books, 2004.

Menashe, Samuel, '*Adam* Means Earth', *New and Selected Poems*, The Library of America, 2005.

C. Murray Rogers, 'Swamiji the Friend' in *Swami Abhishiktānanda: the Man and his Message*, edited by Vandana, ISPK, 2000.

Navajo Indian Prayer, part of the 'Mountain Chant' from *Navajo Myths, Prayers and Song* by Washington Matthews, University of California Press, 1907.

Nin, Anaïs, 'Ragtime' from collection, *Under A Glass Bell*, Editions Poetry London, 1947.

Oliver, Mary, 'The Place I Want to Get Back To' from *Thirst*, Bloodaxe Books, 2006.

O'Donoghue, Bernard, 'In Millstreet Hospital', *Selected Poems*, Faber and Faber, 2008.

O'Driscoll, Ciaran, *A Runner Among Falling Leaves*, Liverpool University Press, 2001.

Rumi, 'The Window Within the Soul', *The Rumi Collection*, Shambhala Publications, Inc., 1998.

Shapcott, Jo, 'Scorpion' from *Of Mutability*, Faber and Faber, 2010.

Smith, Stevie, 'Not Waving but Drowning', *New Selected Poems*, New Directions Publishing Corporation, 1988.

Thomas, R. S., 'Caller', *Poems of R S. Thomas*, University of Arkansas Pr, 1986.

Walcott, Derek, 'Love after Love', *Collected Poems 1948–1984,*Faber and Faber, 1986.

Walser, Robert, 'Snowdrops', *Selected Stories of Robert Walser*, Farrar, Straus, Giroux, 1982.

Warren, Robert Penn, 'Tell Me A Story' in *Slow Time: 100 Poems to Take You There*, editor Niall McMonagle, Marino Books, 2000.

Yeats, W. B., 'Among School Children', *The Poems*, Everyman's Library, 1992.